MW01484736

# BUILDING WEALTH

*From shoeshine boy to real estate magnate*

## ROBERT BARBERA

THE
MENTORIS
PROJECT

The author has made every effort to ensure the accuracy of the information within this book was correct at time of publication. The author does not assume and hereby disclaims any liability to any party for any loss, damage, or disruption caused by errors or omissions, whether such errors or omissions result from accident, negligence, or any other cause.

Barbera Foundation, Inc.
P.O. Box 1019
Temple City, CA 91780

More information at www.mentorisproject.org

ISBN: 978-1-947431-26-3

Library of Congress Control Number: 2019937847

All net proceeds from the sale of this book will be donated to Barbera Foundation, Inc. whose mission is to support educational initiatives that foster an appreciation of history and culture to encourage and inspire young people to create a stronger future.

# CONTENTS

# INTRODUCTION

Wealth isn't about money.

You may be surprised that I'm saying this in a book filled with financial advice, but there is nothing I'm more passionate about sharing than this concept of wealth.

All my adult life, people have asked me, "Robert, how did you make money? How did you become wealthy?" And while I want to share that with them—and with you—I also want you to understand that those are two different questions. Yes, of course, money can help you to create wealth. But wealth is far more than a number on your bank statement.

So if wealth isn't about money, what exactly is it?

Wealth is independence.

Real wealth is the ability to live your life on your own terms. It's the freedom to switch careers, spend time with your children, improve your community, and make a difference in the world. My goal in this book is to help you not only to reach your own financial goals, but also to attain this level of wealth. Attain it and embrace it.

No journey in life is a straight line. You will circle back to different cycles every time you take a new turn. Yes, you will need to start with a Mindset of Wealth, but that doesn't mean you won't need to remind yourself of your commitment and revisit those ideas many times over in your career. Relationships are another thing you must keep building throughout your life, but it's inevitable that there will be moments when you are so engaged in family and business obligations that other valuable relationships will be neglected. Even your vision for your life and your future will evolve over time; you'll need to regroup and refocus again and again for clarity.

This is not meant to discourage you. On the contrary, what I believe—and what I hope to show you in this book—is how real wealth is attainable at any stage of your life. Over the years, we change, circumstances shift, new opportunities continually present themselves. We may need to shore up some foundational elements we thought were taken care of. But we may also find ourselves at any time poised for the next big cycle of wealth.

The principles are here for you. Start where you are.

Enjoy the journey.

# CHAPTER ONE

## THE MINDSET OF WEALTH

Before you can build wealth, you have to build your mindset. This isn't about banishing your negative associations of money or visualizing gold pouring into your life—although by all means feel free to do both if you think it will help. Building your Mindset of Wealth is about training yourself to make the decisions that support the creation of wealth rather than squandering opportunities and resources.

Your mindset is your default response to life. When presented with a new situation, your instinctive reaction is immensely difficult to overcome. If you're terrified of risk, if you spend money to make yourself feel important, if you put off long-term gains for short-term advantages, then your mindset is working against the creation of wealth. While it's not impossible to overcome these tendencies and make better decisions in the moment, it is both painful and exhausting, and it's something you will have to deal with over and over again.

Changing your mindset to one that supports the creation of wealth is a critical first step to relieving that burden. I will tell you what you need to know to create a Mindset of Wealth, but like any muscle, it needs to be exercised. Every day, you should look for opportunities to be self-reliant, to save rather than spend, to assess both risks and potential rewards, and to enjoy the life you already have.

# Learning Self-Reliance

It may sound strange to start a section on self-reliance by talking about how much other people have influenced and helped me, but bear with me. Before we can become self-reliant, we all start out as dependent, not just for food and shelter, but also for guidance on how to see the world. Our defining years are inevitably defined by someone else. For me, my mother and father played pivotal roles, each giving me a different—and ultimately complementary—view of wealth. But it was my brother, Henry, who, throughout my life, exerted a tremendous influence on the man I would become.

Henry was two and a half years older than me, and decades wiser. A brilliant man with a photographic memory and a great and loving heart, he inspired me, believed in me, and watched out for me. Henry taught me how to swim. He taught me how to dance. He opened the doors for me to employment and to college.

But before all of that, Henry taught me how to shine shoes.

My brother and I always worked around the house; family chores earned us money to go to the movies on Saturday. But it wasn't long before we wanted more than family chores could provide. My father was always wonderful with his hands, so he built Henry a solid wooden box for him to carry supplies and use as a footrest for clients while he shined their shoes. Henry started his own business and soon brought me into it. There I went, box in hand, out to Jamaica Avenue in Queens to set up shop.

I was six years old when I started working. I made ten cents for a twenty-minute shoeshine, and I quickly realized the real value of the work I did: Two shoeshines equaled one afternoon at the movies. A couple of extra shoeshines meant candy from the concession stand.

Not to brag too much, but I did a fantastic job shining shoes. First of all, I really enjoyed the work. I gave value for money, shining everything from toe to heel. I even gave it a spit polish. My shoeshine was something to be proud of.

I really believe in that. No matter what you're doing, be proud of your work. Do a complete job; delight your customer. Give real value.

2

If you can be justifiably proud of a shoeshine, you're on your way to great things.

Sometimes I was done in an hour; sometimes it took me all morning just to get one client. At this point, I wasn't thinking about saving or investing, but I was gaining valuable insight into something most kids never know: the power of money to create independence. I didn't have to ask anyone's permission to be able to go to the movies or buy candy or popcorn; I earned the money myself and spent it in the way that gave me the most satisfaction. Even at the age of six, I was living life to a certain degree on my own terms.

I can't stress enough the importance of this single insight. Recognizing at such a young age that earning money was not only something I could do, but that I could decide how to spend it was a defining moment in my life. Money was never something I wanted for itself. It was never associated with status or self-worth in my mind. Instead, money quickly became associated with independence.

This is a tremendously useful mindset when it comes to creating wealth.

I'll never deny that money is useful, but the constant quest for more money, or the use of money as a symbol of status or worth, is a distraction from the ultimate goal of wealth. As I mentioned in the introduction, real wealth is freedom. There is no freedom in chasing money for its own sake. You have to be able to separate your worth from your bank account.

But back to shining shoes. That particular business took me out of my own neighborhood and put me in contact with a different kind of clientele. These were men in suits, men who carried themselves with confidence. Men who—unlike my father, who did everything for himself—were willing and able to pay someone else to shine their shoes.

From them, I learned another important lesson: Money was something I could earn. Some don't learn this until high school, college, or even later. That first job can seem elusive; many people think of working for someone else as the only way to make a buck.

But I started working for myself at the age of six. All it took was ingenuity, desire, and a secondhand shoeshine box. I grew up knowing that earning money was always *possible*—although I'm not saying it was always easy. There was competition from older boys, bad weather meant no customers, and as I was underage and unlicensed, I was often chased away by the police. In fact, my shoe-shining days ended when a cop smashed my box with his baton and nearly smashed my leg in the process. But despite the setbacks, I remained secure in the knowledge that there were things I could do in the world that were of value, that other people would pay me for.

# Henry's Legacy

There was another way in which Henry had a profound impact on me. It was during the last week of his life. I was driving Henry to the hospital for what turned out to be the last time.

"Bobby," he said, "I could have done more with my talents. I could have done more with my life."

Let me tell you, this is not something you want to hear from someone you love. And it's certainly not something you ever want to have to say yourself. Hearing this, I realized I had always assumed that Henry was living the life he wanted. And it was a good life—I don't want to take away from that. But in the end, his greatest regret was that he hadn't done more with what he'd been given. And mine was that I hadn't helped him to do more.

That conversation made me double down on my commitment to help others. If Henry had been honest with himself about what he really wanted from life when there was still time, who knows what he might have accomplished? Many times in this book, I'm going to ask you to be brutally honest with yourself, now, before it's too late to act. You don't have to share your insights with anyone else; they are private and personal. But you have to be completely honest with yourself about what you want and what's stopping you from reaching those goals. Your first step is to be honest about your perception of both money and your ability to earn it.

## Money as Independence

The key to the Mindset of Wealth is recognizing money as independence. We all want to have power and agency over our own lives, and money is one of the components that makes that possible. If you think of money as synonymous with your personal worth or status, you're going to miss out on opportunities to exchange money for joy—or even for more money, through smart investments that may nonetheless involve risk. Money for its own sake is not the path to wealth.

Start with recognizing your perception of money and look for ways to shift it toward the concept of independence. How can the money you already have free you from something onerous? How can it add value and joy to your life right now, today? I'm not saying quit your job or book a trip you can't afford, but I do want you to do something small that makes the relationship between money and independence real to you. It can be as small as going to a movie or perhaps paying someone else to shine your shoes. Whatever it is, be very aware of the joy and/or the sense of freedom that the experience gives you. Recognize that it's the *experience* giving you that joy, not the money itself. Money is only a facilitator.

But the Mindset of Wealth is not only equating money with independence. It's also recognizing that you have agency. You are capable of living the life you want. Self-reliance is an important skill set, and if you weren't lucky enough to learn it at six, you need to learn it as soon as you can. If you want to be wealthy, you have to start by being on top of your own needs, earning your own money, making your own decisions. The confidence of being self-reliant feeds on itself, and confidence in your own abilities is a critical component of building wealth.

## Have a Big Vision

My mother, Rosalina, was an ambitious woman. She had a gift for negotiations, for understanding people and their needs, and above all, for real estate. Although she had little in the way of formal education, she had a firm grasp of business essentials. When I was thirteen, World War II was just winding down and my mother realized we were on the verge of a new era. Soldiers were going to be coming home, getting married, needing a place to live.

She asked my dad for $200 to fix the roof. Instead, she used the money to put a down payment on a vacant lot in Jamaica Estates in Queens.

My mother, who had only a third-grade education, turned to me to read the contracts to her. I would sit on the top stair outside her bedroom while she was getting dressed and read the contracts aloud to her. Sometimes, I'd have to explain some of the words. But my mother didn't just listen; she memorized. She understood the numbers and she was a hard negotiator. She would walk into the room knowing exactly what was in those contracts and she would make sure she got the best possible deal. Meanwhile, I learned all about contracts and the language of business from those early years.

My mother partnered with a contractor to build three duplexes. Without telling my father, she put our house on the market. We moved into a rooming house and she used the money from the sale of our house to finance the first duplex. When she sold that, she used that money for the second duplex, and then repeated the process to finance the third. We moved into that last duplex, but only until she could parlay the other properties she'd bought into a thirty-unit apartment building in Richmond Hill. Finally, we moved into that building, as owners and landlords.

Even that didn't last, however. My mother sold the Richmond Hill property to buy a sixty-unit apartment building in Brooklyn, which itself ended up financing two tracts of homes back in Queens. She was doing tremendously well financially, but my father had had enough. My mother could tolerate an endless amount of risk—and such an ambitious project was not without setbacks. There were lawsuits, there were tenants who refused to pay, and then there was the uprooting of our family. My father hated living in an apartment, and the added pressures of the financial and legal risks were too much for him. My parents separated.

While I'm much more like my mother than I am like my father—particularly when it comes to my tolerance for risk—I have a lot of both of my parents in me. And I was able to learn not just from their example, but from their successes and failures.

Here are the two key things I learned from my mother:

- Set a goal. Use it to leapfrog to the next goal.
- Everything in life is a negotiation.

And the two key things I learned from my father:

- Wealth is about more than money.
- Know your value.

## The Importance of Goals

It's almost impossible to talk about my mother without talking about goals. Everything Rosalina did was in service to a bigger picture. When she and my father were first married, she defied him to work outside the home because she wanted to save enough money so they could buy their own factory. When they lost that factory in the Depression, she did it again, sneaking out to work so that ultimately they could buy their second factory. And you've already read how she parlayed one vacant lot into bigger and better properties. Everything she achieved was a stepping stone to a larger vision.

My mother set a big goal for herself. She had a vision for her life and she was willing to work hard for it. But she also worked smart. She saw the steps she could take to make the vision come true, and she used each success to propel her to the next success.

This also made it easier for her—and later for me—to view every job not as merely a paycheck, but as an opportunity. Every job has its downside. The work can be boring or beneath your abilities or exhausting, or all of those things. If you just see it as an exchange of your time and energy for money, any job will quickly become onerous. But if

7

instead you see what you're doing as a stepping stone to an important personal goal, it not only makes it easier to bear, but also opens up possibilities to make the job itself more interesting and useful.

For instance, it's a long tradition that Hollywood agents start their careers in the mailroom. Consequently, literary and talent agencies have mailrooms filled with smart, college-educated men and women doing the most menial of tasks. Why would these young people do this? They could be very much in demand in corporate America, yet they're working below their potential for little more than minimum wage. And these jobs are competitive, with hundreds of overqualified applicants vying for each opening. Why?

Because they rightly see it as a stepping stone to the big vision of their career as a Hollywood agent. The experience of learning the business from the bottom up, the relationships they make, the negotiations they're privy to—these are worth far more to them than a paycheck.

I'm not saying you should become a Hollywood agent, of course, but I do suggest that you see your current job as a pathway to your big vision. And I know you have a big vision or you never would have picked up this book.

Think big, take small steps to get there, and wring the most out of each situation.

## The Art of Negotiation

In addition to having vision, my mother was a tough negotiator. She went into real estate at a time when almost everyone she would be dealing with was a man. This was not a world in which women were expected to be savvy. Also, as I mentioned, she had a third-grade education, and English wasn't her native language and she had never taken a business class. There were a lot of people just waiting to take advantage of her.

What my mother taught me is that in order to negotiate, you first have to understand exactly what's going on. What is being negotiated, who are the players, how does the business operate, what's the bottom line you need to be successful? Remember, I read her those contracts over and over again; she memorized the numbers, she understood the risks and the possible rewards. She overcame all the strikes against her by being the most prepared person in the room—and by knowing exactly what she wanted and what she was willing to give up to get it.

But my mother was also fair. In my own business dealings, I've always looked to create a win-win. Perhaps it comes from watching what happened when negotiations between my own parents broke down and they had to separate. I believe in preparation and in knowing what you want and going for it, but I also believe in making sure everyone leaves the room with something that matters to them.

Which takes us to my father.

## Wealth Is More than Money

My father, John, was less ambitious than my mother, but I don't mean to imply that he was any less successful. They simply had different definitions of success.

Dad was an artist, a fashion designer. He had worked his way up from sweeping the floor of a garment factory, learning every aspect of the business. He was so highly sought after that he could work during the fashion "season" and then take several months off. He would listen to opera, read widely, drink good wine—in other words, he would thoroughly enjoy the life he had. My father was talented and accomplished, and he worked very hard. But he also fully enjoyed life. He had a sense of "enough."

This is something that is missing from so much of our lives today. Everyone, it seems, is pushing constantly; the messages all seem to be *work harder, move faster, be better*. While in temperament, I am driven like my mother was, my father's example had a lasting influence on me and I'm grateful for it.

My father taught me that wealth was not only money.

Money was important. My dad spent his life developing his skills, learning the garment business, and making the most of his innate talent. When it was time to work, he gave it his all despite a grueling pace. But when the season was over, he rested. He would work flat out as a fashion designer for three months, and then didn't work again for the next nine. He didn't wait until he had retired to enjoy the fruits of his labor. And that down time gave him the chance to explore other talents. He relished working with his hands, fixing and building things. He was a tremendous cook. He refurbished the houses my mother bought. He liked making things beautiful. All of this demanded time and patience rather than money. Dad filled his days with the life he wanted, fully experiencing both the demanding work and the replenishing rest.

My dad was at peace with himself, and he showed me what it was to be satisfied.

I like to work. I like to have a side project going, I like to learn about a new business, I like to keep busy. But my father's example showed me that there is great value in enjoying what you already have. It can renew your focus. It can help you discover new interests. It might even lead to a side business. But it doesn't have to lead to a paycheck to be valuable. We only get one life. It's important to enjoy the journey.

## Know Your Value

The other important lesson my dad taught me was to know my own value. When I said he was in high demand, I wasn't exaggerating. He was a fashion creator and he reached the pinnacle of success in his field. Garment factories would come to him and offer him fabulous sums to teach their staff how to do what he did. He always refused. He would patiently explain that this was his talent, his ability; even if he could teach someone else the art of how he designed, he didn't want to.

Don't give yourself away. Know the value of what you do. I'm not saying don't mentor others; in fact, I'm a big believer in mentorship and will have more on that later in the book. What I'm saying is don't sell yourself short. Don't assume by default that if you can do it, anyone can. Work hard, build your skills, refine your talents. And then be prepared to ask for what you want and be paid for what you're worth.

# Own Your Destiny

It's important to recognize that the small decisions you make every day have a lasting impact on your life. If you want to be wealthy, you have to make decisions that will support that. These are probably different decisions than the ones you're making now.

For instance, credit cards. I've seen people buy a cup of coffee with a credit card instead of cash. This is a terrible idea! First of all, if you're not paying the entire balance off every month, that coffee costs you more because you're paying interest on it—money that could go to building the life you want. But even if you do pay off your balance every time, I'm still not a believer in credit cards because they give you a sense that you have more money than you actually do. It's hard to build a budget and stick with it when you don't see the money passing through your hands.

At one point in the 1970s, I was asked to speak to a church group, to the women of the congregation, about money. Women, as the stewards of their family's budget, were also the keepers of the credit cards. And one of the things I asked them to do was to hand over all their credit cards to me, so that I could destroy them.

I was not very popular.

It's forty years later, but my message hasn't changed. You might not like to hear it any more than they did, but I promise you, it is life changing. Credit cards work against you. They encourage you to spend more, they penalize you heavily if you fail to pay them off in full every single month, and they prevent you from seeing that each purchase is a decision that has a real impact on your wallet. Taking on a business loan is one thing; scrambling financially in your personal life is something else entirely.

Happiness is being on top of your money. Being independent is freedom. Sure, credit cards are convenient, but if you're not willing to trade a little inconvenience now for a wealthy and secure future, put the book down now. I can't help you. You have to be able to see that the choices you make now are setting you up for either future success or future failure.

What do you actually want from life? I want freedom. I've always wanted it. I wanted to be able to make decisions because they were right for me, not because I was shackled to a paycheck. That meant building my skills, trying new things, getting an education, but above all, it meant being unburdened by debt.

I have been able to take advantage of tremendous opportunities in my life, even when they came with a smaller paycheck, because of this philosophy. We think we always keep going up and up, but that's not true. If you change careers, if you find something else you're passionate about, if you realize that an additional skill set would set you apart, sometimes you need to go back to school, or to start over somewhere else and take a pay cut. I never hesitated to start at the bottom rung if it was a good opportunity—and I didn't have to hesitate, because my wife, Bernice, and I never burdened ourselves by taking on personal debt. I've grown from every opportunity; like my mother, I've been able to parlay one thing into another. But it hasn't always been easy, or a straight path. Being saddled with personal debt—having to make decisions based on fear and the pressing need for a paycheck, rather than on possibility and security—would have made my journey harder, if not impossible.

Beyond giving you the breathing room to make good decisions, embracing stewardship of your finances is foundational. In the next chapter, I'm going to talk about the power of savings and the importance of living below your means. All I ask from you now is that you try it. If you're not already debt-free, make it your primary goal to get there. The peace of mind that you'll feel when debt is no longer hanging over your head is the first step toward real wealth.

## No Excuses

This is your life. You only get one shot at this. Excuses are not acceptable. I'm not saying you have to make a million dollars to be successful—what I am saying is that once you figure out what success means to you, you have to commit to it fully. Don't let yourself off the hook. Live the life you want to live, whether it's working flat out for three months and cooking and listening to opera for the other nine, or relentlessly sewing practically 24/7 to build an investment fund.

Don't compare yourself to others. There will always be someone with more money, more success, more talent, more genius than you. What does that matter? It has no impact at all on your life. All that matters is that you deliberately live the life you want fully and with the people you love, so that when the end comes, you can look back and have no regrets.

And you may just make a million while doing it.

# RECAP: THE MINDSET OF WEALTH

- **Money is not wealth.** Money is one tool to help build a life of wealth, but it's not important for its own sake, only for what it can do for you.

- **You are capable of creating value that others will pay you for.** If a six-year-old can make money as an entrepreneur, you certainly can.

- **Have a Big Vision.** Leverage your current goal to leapfrog to your next goal.

- **Be honest with yourself about your tolerance for risk.** Minimize risk with due diligence, research, and preparation, but understand that nothing is entirely risk-free.

- **Appreciate and enjoy what you already have.**

- **Your expertise makes you valuable.** Don't give it away.

- **Get out of debt.** Cut up your credit cards, avoid retail therapy, and feel the happiness and freedom that financial security brings.

- **Don't compare yourself to anyone else.** Live your life, your way. Make the most of your talents and your opportunities; don't get caught up in either envy or arrogance.

# CHAPTER TWO

## LAYING THE FOUNDATION

I'll tell you the truth: Most people want to get rich by winning the lottery. They want an easy solution that requires no effort and little outlay. Of course, what most people don't realize is that winning the lottery is no guarantee of a lifetime of wealth. In fact, many lottery winners end up broke within a few years. The same is true of athletes with million-dollar salaries, A-list actors, heirs to family fortunes—almost anyone who receives a sudden windfall is vulnerable to losing it all. Why is that?

Because they haven't developed a foundation that supports wealth.

What I mean by that is they haven't been taught how to manage their money. And the time to learn is before you have a lot of it; money can bring complications as well as opportunities. You need a solid foundation in place both to build wealth and to deal with it once you have it.

I honestly don't know why schools don't teach money management early, right alongside math and reading. The ability to read a contract and to understand what it means for your future, the ability to develop a budget and not have to scramble to pay the bills every month—these things are as foundational to a successful life as understanding chemistry or discussing history or speaking a second language. Maybe more so.

While I can't change the national curriculum, I can educate you about the critical things you need to be able to do. And we're going to start with the single most important piece you'll need to master to transform your life.

We're going to start with a budget.

# Understanding Your Budget

Your budget is your financial lifeline. It's not just about how much you have for groceries, it's about making sure you have enough to build a business and launch your dreams. I don't just want you to budget—I want you to *love* to budget. I want you to embrace your personal or family budget as the key to your future success.

If you can't budget a household, you can't budget a business.

Start with the numbers. Numbers provide clarity. You may have been avoiding looking at them because they don't seem to you to be impressive enough. You may not be bringing in as much money as you want to; you may think that a low income is a reflection of your worth as a person. Nothing could be further from the truth. When I shined shoes for ten cents a polish, I never saw my worth as being tied to the money I made. On the contrary, my self-confidence was increased by the fact that I was making my own money, however small the amount, and by the pride I took in the job I did.

Numbers are your friends. Knowing your actual income and outgo is the first step toward gaining control over your financial life. As long as you remain ignorant about your financial situation, you can kiss any thought of wealth goodbye.

It might help to think of your budget as the budget of a business: You, Inc. Whatever it takes to shake off the emotional baggage that's keeping you from honestly assessing your financial situation, do it. The stakes are that high.

# Outgo

To start with, take a look at where you spend your money. Some financial advisers suggest keeping a notebook and tracking every purchase for a month, and that's great. Don't let me stop you if you want to run with it. But I don't really want you to wait a month before getting some numbers in front of your eyes. For the most part, your fixed expenses don't change all that much, and that's where I want you to start.

How much do you pay in rent or mortgage? What about utilities? Insurance? Property taxes? These are your fixed costs. If they fluctuate—heating costs, for instance, are far more in December than they are in July—then grab your bills for the past year, add them up, and divide by twelve to get a monthly average. (If you don't keep physical bills, don't worry; we live in the age where everything is online, so check your account.) Phone, college loan repayments, money you send home to your mother—whatever you do every month, write it down. I'm not asking you to evaluate, trim, refinance, or judge here. Just get the numbers on a piece of paper.

Chances are this is not all you spend in a month. If you commute to work, for instance, you need to buy metro tickets or put gas in the car. That kind of expense is necessary. Dinner out on Friday nights, not as much. Grab your credit card statements—because despite my strong suggestion, I'll bet you still haven't cut up your credit cards yet—and take a look at where the money went. Groceries, coffee, dinner with friends, movies. Again, I'm not judging and I don't want you to; not yet, anyway. Just get it all down, each in its own category.

Total it up. Now you have a ballpark for your monthly expenses.

## Income

Now take a look at your income. This is usually pretty simple. Most people have one paycheck every two weeks. Even if you have an extra job or part-time income, you can pretty much rely on a certain amount every month. If you work for yourself, your income can vary, sometimes spectacularly, as my father's did. If that's true for you, total up your annual income and divide by twelve. You want real numbers to work from.

# Income Over Expenses

I am hoping that you have a positive number when you subtract your expenses from your income. If you don't, then this is your first priority, fixing this immediate situation. I have some ideas that I'll talk about later in this chapter, but I can't stress this enough: You are never going to be wealthy until you control your finances. If you're in the red—and even if you're just skating close to the red—your finances are controlling you. You can't create wealth when you're scrambling to make rent.

My mother understood this. Despite my father's objections, she insisted on working outside the home. Let's be clear: This was not so that we could go on lavish summer vacations. My mother sewed piecework—constantly, because she was paid by the piece—so that she and my father could buy a garment factory. And after they lost the first factory in the Great Depression, she did it again so that they could buy their second factory.

Did you get that? My mother raised the extra money needed to buy a factory with one piece of sewing at a time.

Don't tell me that it was a different era, because I guarantee you that women seamstresses have never been a highly paid workforce. And sure, my father's income also went to the factory, but it was also what we all lived on. It would have taken far longer for my parents to build their business without that extra income.

You may need a second job. I myself have never been without what the kids today call a "side hustle." I recommend it for a lot of reasons, all of which I'll discuss in a minute. But before we go into ways to supplement your income, you first need to go back and look at all those expenses.

# Living Beneath Your Means

This is where I'm going to ask you to make some hard decisions. This is also where you have the power to immediately change your life.

When my wife, Bernice, and I first got married, I was going to college while she worked full-time. Eventually, I was able to get some scholarships to lighten the burden, but we didn't have a lot of money kicking around. And it was never our plan to be a two-income household; Bernice was putting me through college so that I could get a better job and we could start a family. Money wasn't in our present or our immediate future.

That didn't mean we didn't have fun.

What we did do was make the decision that our future was just as important as our present. I knew right away that Bernice wasn't someone who needed the high life to be happy: Our first date was going to church during Holy Week to see the Stations of the Cross. The first time I took her out to dinner, she ordered a cheese sandwich, the cheapest thing on the menu. We weren't even really a couple yet, and already Bernice was watching out for me financially. When we did get married—I was ready the moment I met her, but she made me wait six months—we had a great time doing things on the cheap or for free, because we were together. We went on a lot of walks. We had picnics in the park. We didn't even go to the movies— we stayed home and watched TV, but we never felt deprived.

We were building a future together. Even on only one paycheck and paying for college, we still put a big chunk of Bernice's salary into our savings account. When I held a day job, I told my family that we were going to live off of my salary. Anything else—anything from side jobs or from our investments—all of that money went into savings to be reinvested either into the business or into a better opportunity. We budgeted for everything, including food, and we stuck to that budget. You can look at anything in life as either a deprivation or an opportunity. Bernice and I always saw our finances as a way to build our future, and we raised our children on that philosophy. Just like with art, having some restrictions forces you to think creatively. For us, our budget compelled us to find creative ways to have fun together.

Remember how much my father enjoyed life? A glass of wine, a record playing, a good book and he was a happy man. He took great joy in cooking dinner, and he was a terrific cook, better than my mom, because he loved it so much. You can start living a life of wealth right now by choosing to do the things you love that don't cost much money.

It sounds simple, and it is. Living below your means is true freedom because it takes worrying about money right out of the equation. It's far more satisfying and easier to sustain than trying to buy happiness with a credit card.

You can rail against it or you can embrace it, but living below your means is the only way to build the savings you will need to take risks, grow a business, and succeed financially. And it's certainly the only way to make sure that you keep your money once you've got it.

## Compound Interest Is Your Friend

The basic rule of wealth is to let your resources compound. If you stuff your money in a mattress, okay, you'll have a bed of money, but what you won't have going for you is the power of compound interest. This is when your money gets interest and the interest is added into the principal so that it, too, can earn interest. Reinvesting dividends in stocks is similar in that you end up with more shares that can earn more for you as the stocks go up.

Reinvesting profits into your business falls along similar lines. Buying more efficient machinery, investing in education for your workforce that will allow them to be more effective, buying a new building or upgrading an existing one so that you can be at the top of the rental scales—these are all ways to have your money work for you. But the mindset starts with understanding and seeking out ways to grow your savings with compound interest at the best possible rates.

## Time

You also need to budget your time. There are more things you *could* do than you have time to do. You need to set priorities within your business. What can you do that no one else can do? Focus your attention there. What is urgent? What is important? There is a difference, and you often need to juggle both. There's a lot of stress involved in running a business and much of it revolves around not having enough time to do all the things that need to be done, or—more critically—to even consider all the things that need to be considered. There have been a couple of times in my life where I moved too quickly, where I didn't think through the best use of my resources. Having a little extra time is like having that cushion of money, and you get it the same way, but relentlessly cutting out the things that cost you time with no return.

Of course, you could also go sit down and watch TV rather than spend that time putting together a marketing plan for your new product. If this sounds like I'd vastly prefer you write up the plan, well, you're right. I would. But it's not my life we're talking about, it's yours. You have to make the choice. I want you to make choices that lead to a good life, a wealthy life. If you were to tell me that watching that particular TV show was a conscious decision because it's time you spend together with your family once a week—okay, now you have my attention. What you choose to spend time on reflects your values like nothing else, even more than what you spend money on. I'm just saying, weigh your options. Be deliberate.

## Education

I grew up in a different era than children today. When I was in elementary school, only one in four Americans ended up with a high school diploma. Far fewer went on to college. But in our family, there was never any question: My parents had high expectations. Ultimately, both my brother and I didn't just finish high school, but also went on to college. In fact, Henry got his PhD, taught college, wrote books, and mastered French, German, and Italian. It was certainly far beyond what was expected of us—of anyone, really—when we were kids.

My parents understood the importance of education. My mother had only gone as far as third grade; while she appreciated having me to read contracts to her, she would rather have been able to read them for herself. And both she and my father understood how essential math was to everything we wanted to do in life.

If you're still in school, get a solid education. You will never regret it. It's not about the letter grade, it's about mastery. Letter grades, in my experience, have been a poor predictor of success in life. But if you learn not just how to read, but how to understand what you read, you're in good shape. Make sure you have a solid grasp of math, including accounting. Learning how to read a proposal and see what's missing, or how to keep the books—those are such basic skills to being successful financially, it's akin to learning the alphabet. Take night classes, go online, hire a tutor, do whatever you need to do to come out the other end confident in your ability to understand the building blocks of the business world. My mother understood every word of the contracts I read to her. She did the math in her head. She ran circles around the lawyers and businessmen in every negotiation. Confidence and mastery go hand in hand, and each one supports the other.

I did poorly in high school, at least at first. Although I did well in math in college, back in high school, I couldn't see the practicality of algebra and I failed it. I had to take a world language, and my Italian kept popping up in the middle of Spanish class. But high school was of immense importance to me not in spite of, but because of, those failures. I switched from an academic diploma to a commercial one, and it made all the difference. For the first time, I was taking business courses, including bookkeeping. I loved these courses and I did very well in them. These classes were practical and I could see how they would help me become the person I wanted to be. Explore your options, take a variety of classes, see where you shine. Again, it's not the grades that matter, but mastery and direction. You only get one life, so make sure it's going where you want it to go.

When I started working, it was for General Electric Credit Corporation. I wanted to put those high school business courses to work. I started as a messenger, but pretty soon I was a file clerk and then a reconciliation accountant. The lightbulb moment for me came when I realized that another guy doing roughly the same work I did was making a lot more money. Why? Because he had gone to college. Right there, I made the decision that I was going to get my college degree. It was an excellent decision, both for the education and for the relationships I made.

Beyond what you can learn through formal education, there is another education I want you to go after. Go out into the world. Move around. Learn from everyone. This is the second education: the education of employment, of a business career.

The more you know, the more you realize what you do not know. Change is constant, and you have to be able to spot opportunities when they present themselves—and also realize when something is winding down. The advent of the motor car effectively ended the booming industry in carriage-building. Individuals who invested in themselves by learning how to fix these new engines found they were in high demand; those who only knew how to repair carriage wheels had some hard years ahead.

Like school, this second education can also encompass finding out where your talents lie. You may think you want to go into the restaurant business. Maybe, like my dad, you love to cook. Maybe you've even taken cooking classes and (I trust) a good course in accounting so you understand the books. Going and getting an actual job in the kind of restaurant you want to own will be a revelation to you. Work the front of the house at one place, work the hot line at another. See the hours the owner puts in, and what they actually do. You may ultimately decide that you do want to be a chef, or maybe you want to manage the restaurant, or maybe you discover a love of public relations and decide you want to specialize in PR for restaurants. You won't learn the reality of any business and where your particular skill set meshes with that industry's needs until you have worked in that world.

## Working for Someone Else

A lot of books out there today suggest you can find financial success by following your passion, working only a few hours a week, and quitting your day job. It sounds great, but it's not what you'll find here in this book because those things do not, in my experience, automatically lead to success. Bernice and I traded off on holding day jobs to make sure the rent was paid and food made it to the table, and there have been times in my life when I've worked every possible hour in the day. When it comes to following your passion, well, there you have me, because I have followed mine. I have always been driven to be financially successful, and I've enjoyed every bit of my life along the way. Just don't expect passion alone to get you there.

But back to day jobs. There are advantages to working for someone else. For one thing, you don't have to be the one to rustle up the clients. A paycheck arrives on time, every couple of weeks. Money is paid into your social security and taxes. I held a regular nine-to-five job for much of my life, and as a way to learn about a business or industry, meet your financial obligations, save for the future, and—especially—meet people in your field, working in an established company is peerless.

It also provides you with the opportunity to get better at the skills you will need to run your own business. For instance, way back when I was delivering newspapers, my brother and I showed up on time, every day. You won't be surprised to learn that not every elementary school kid is that consistent and reliable. The newspaper dealer was so impressed with us that he gave us more routes. Not only did that mean more papers and more money, but these were also much better routes in high-rises, which meant more deliveries in a shorter time. I learned at a very young age that just showing up on time every day helped me to stand out, and that I was rewarded for that. And you know what? I've found that to be true my entire life. Being consistent and reliable is a foundational skill, and if it's one you struggle with, let me suggest you start working on it. We're going to talk later about your reputation and how that can help or hinder your business deals and ultimately your success, and being reliable is the cornerstone of a good reputation. Start small, but start today.

Working for someone else is particularly valuable when you're trying to get a foot in the door of a new industry. My father started by sweeping floors in a garment factory and worked his way through every level until he was at the very top. I never minded taking a pay cut and starting over at the bottom if it meant learning about a new business. Part of that was self-confidence; I knew I had something to offer every employer, and I wasn't going to be stuck at the bottom for long. But it was also that I understood the value of learning about the realities of the business rather than coming in mid-level with big ideas and no scaffolding on which to pin them. Seeing the problems faced by your staff, your sales team, and your customers can only lead to more creative, on-point, and successful solutions. If you're going to climb the ladder of any industry, starting at the bottom rung gives you the firmest foundation.

There's another plus to working for someone else: It gives you an automatic way into the relationships that dominate any business. You meet colleagues, you meet suppliers, you meet customers, and you meet them all with the weight of an established company behind you. Relationships are such an important piece for you to develop that I'll be talking about it in depth in the next chapter.

Most of all, when you work for someone else, you learn how to please both the boss and the customer. You also learn to handle your fellow employees. Too many employees speak ill of their employers; don't be one of them. It's important to learn to balance your professional relationships with your peers with your professional obligations to both your employer and your clients. Most of life is spent navigating between people with different agendas and ideally making them all happy. In addition, how you deal with others—with grace, I hope, and with integrity—is a tremendous factor in your success. When you're working for someone else, that is a skill you are forced to develop, working with other people and even learning to be the go-between who makes other relationships run smoothly. It is a very good skill to have.

Be open to learning whatever the job can teach you. Look for the foundational skills—how to negotiate, how to listen, what is valued within that business or community—as well as specific skills such as learning to read contracts, balancing the books, or understanding project designs. Nowadays, there seems to be a specific software for every business imaginable; teaching yourself on the job is as good as graduate school, and instead of shelling out tuition, they're paying you to do it.

## Working on the Side

You already know that I was my own boss by the age of six—at least until the policeman smashed my shoeshine box. But I didn't stop there. During World War II, Henry and I went around the neighborhood picking up old papers and scrap metal, which we sold to the salvage yard. After the war, we did grounds work, shoveling snow in the winter and cutting grass and pulling weeds in the summer. Small though I was, I caddied at the golf course. And Bernice and I managed our apartment buildings while I was still working full-time and she was raising the kids. All my life, I've been earning my own money on my own time with some kind of side businesses.

I'm a big believer in doing something where you are your own boss. Your day job may be working for someone else, or maybe you're still in school, but there are many advantages to working for yourself on the side.

For one thing, you learn valuable skills. As a young boy, I delivered newspapers and learned all about collections when clients didn't want to pay for their subscriptions. This was a skill my mother would count on in the coming years when she'd send me to talk to tenants who were late on their rent. You also learn about time management. You've heard the saying, "If you want something done, ask a busy woman"? When you have a lot on your plate, you learn to make the most of every minute. Henry and I managed our jobs, school, homework, friends, sports, and family time. It's a skill I use to this day.

There's a pride, too, that comes from managing your own time and directly seeing how what you do—or what you choose not to do—impacts your bottom line. It's also a way to try out new avenues and pick up new skills, especially when you're young and you're not yet sure what kind of work will be fulfilling.

And then of course there's the money. You will need capital to fund your business, and to do that, you will need to sock away as much money as you can. I'm going to repeat myself, but living below your means is the smartest decision you will ever make. Putting a chunk—as big a chunk as you can—of your paycheck into your savings will give you the financial foundation you need to start or grow your business, make your first real estate deal, take a necessary risk in your career. Supplementing that with income from a side business will enable you to pursue your goals that much faster.

One of the key things to understand with any business, whether you're working for yourself or for someone else, is that nothing lasts forever. The shoe-shining business ended with a broken box (and nearly a broken leg; I was lucky that the box took the brunt of the police officer's blow), our salvage endeavors ended with the war, and I've ultimately had half a dozen jobs or more come to an end, usually leading to a move on to something better.

Today this ability to move on to a better prospect is called "pivoting." In my youth, we called it common sense. I was a caddie at an elite golf course; this was a formative experience for me, as it made crystal clear the divide between the golfers and the caddies. I knew right then which side I wanted to be on. As I caddied, I noticed that if the ball went wrong on the fifteenth or sixteenth hole, there was a good chance it would sail over the fence. Henry and I would scramble around after the match was over, looking for lost balls. If they were still in pretty good shape, we could sell them for five or ten cents each to another golfer the next day. I was pretty quick to do the cost-benefit analysis (numbers again!) and it was clear we could make more money for less work by retrieving balls than by caddying. You can call it a pivot; I call it one of the easiest decisions I ever made.

No matter what your situation, be eager to learn and quick to help, but always be looking for your next opportunity.

## RECAP: LAYING THE FOUNDATION

- **Set a budget.** With personal finances, knowledge is power.

- **Live beneath your means.** Scrambling to pay the bills is the antithesis of living a wealthy life.

- **Challenge yourself to live creatively on your budget.** Enjoy the life you're already living.

- **Build your self-confidence by finishing what you start and mastering what you need to learn.**

- **Learn to read, and to understand what you've read.** Contracts can support your success or create pitfalls that can sabotage your future.

- **Get over any fear of math.** The power of numbers is foundational to every business.

- **Get the education you need to do not just your own job, but your next job.** This means challenging yourself to keep learning all the time.

- **Show up.** Be consistent and reliable in everything you do.

- **Be open to learning whatever the job can teach you.**

- **Look for opportunities everywhere**. When you see a better opportunity, take it.

# Chapter Three

## Relationships

You know when I said I didn't get fantastic grades in high school? There was one exception to that: I was an A+ student when it came to socializing.

One of the most important things we learn in high school is how to get along with people who are different from us. Back then, we had fraternities in high school and I joined Alpha Kappa Psi. I come from a family of Italian immigrants, and one of the defining features of our household was food—good Italian food. When one of my fraternity brothers invited me to his house for dinner, I was in for a dose of culture shock. The family wasn't Italian and neither was the food. His mother started ladling stew into our bowls, and at first I thought it was a fraternity prank or even an initiation ritual. You might laugh, but think for a moment what stew looks like: all those ingredients, carrots and beef and onions, mixed together with a gravy-like consistency. I'd never seen anything like it. I watched to make sure my fraternity brother was eating it before I gave it a try, just in case. But I did try it, and it was good. Different, but good. And that's how I felt about all my friends who came from other cultures and backgrounds. We were all different—but good.

Another thing I saw from my friends was how they interacted with their families. Beyond the food, what else went on at the dinner table?

How did people talk to each other? What were their expectations? What could I learn from seeing how other people interacted, based on their own experiences, cultures, and interests? It was tremendously eye-opening as a teenager to realize that my experiences with my parents were not universal. Everyone had a different kind of family and a different way of relating. And of course it was invaluable to learn that your friends can be from wildly different backgrounds and still be loyal and funny and great fraternity brothers. I was lucky to live in New York and be able to go to school with people outside of the culture I knew, and even to shine shoes or caddy for men who were far richer than my parents. Meeting them, listening to them talk—it all pointed the way for me to recognize where I wanted to go. Just knowing they existed changed my future.

You're going to find smart, interesting people everywhere in the world. You're going to find people who have the life you want to lead. Make the most of it. Learn what works for them and see if it works for you. Watch what doesn't work and avoid making the same mistakes. Whenever possible, become colleagues and friends. Every relationship has the potential to be life-altering.

## The Value of Building Relationships

I love people. I've always loved people. Everyone is interesting, everyone has something to offer. But I also believe that our relationships must be beneficial to our development. There's no point maintaining relationships with people who are only using us or drain our energy or pointlessly make our lives more difficult. And yes, I've worked with people like that—and I've quit working with people like that. My "silent" partner in a restaurant that I turned around was anything but silent. Every Monday he would bring me his wife's recommendations—and her complaints. He was difficult to deal with and she was impossible, and ultimately I realized it wasn't worth the hassle. Remember, my goal is to lead a great life, not just make money. I got out of it, not because of the work or the financial rewards, but because of the relationship.

I'm not telling you this story because I want you to be wary of relationships. On the contrary, I want you to get out there and meet people and have lots of great relationships. I just want you to recognize, and be willing to end, relationships that don't serve your goals. And look at the bright side as well: My relationship with even this partner, while it had to end for my own well-being, still led to great success at our restaurant. I learned a lot from managing that business. Every step leads to the next success.

## Meeting People in Your Industry

It's important to know who the players are in your industry. Find out what companies are doing the kind of work you do, or that you want to do. See what professional associations exist in your field. Read the trade magazines—today, a lot of that is online—and keep up with the key players. Above all, look to see who is doing what in your own neighborhood. I can't stress enough the value of showing up and meeting people in person.

In classes and workshops, you can meet people who are at the same level as you are and do the same kind of work. That's great. These are your colleagues. But you also want to meet people who do different jobs within the same industry. The more you understand how the entire business works, the better you'll be able to take advantage of opportunities and make suggestions that grow the company. You'll also be better placed to start your own business someday if you are training yourself in how other departments work.

I mentioned that I was never afraid to start at the bottom if it meant a great opportunity. Sometimes, the opportunity is itself the chance to see how the entire business works. Learn as much as you can and make friends with people at every level.

## Looking for Clients

When you run your own business, you are always looking for clients.

The problem is that a lot of people don't think about it in terms of actually going out and looking for them. They rely too much on marketing or word of mouth. But nothing grows your business like personal connections.

Take a trucker, for instance. When I was working for a credit union, a truck driver came to me wanting to improve his ability to take care of his family. I suggested he make friends with businesspeople who wanted trucking service; when he had several possible clients, he should buy his own truck. The credit union I was managing would lend him money to buy the truck. When he had that going, I suggested he keep on going. In the space of three years, he had several drivers, a mechanic, and a bookkeeper. His wife handled the orders and routed the drivers. This was a man who profoundly changed his life by making personal connections with potential clients.

We want to hire people we already know and like. Be that person and meet people you might be able to help. And then do a great job for them.

## Making Contacts Outside Your Industry

You shouldn't be too focused on just one industry. Remember that the only constant is change. Over my lifetime, I've worked for the IRS, managed a credit union and a restaurant, consulted with CPAs, sold life insurance, worked as a Blue Cross auditor, ran an automobile dealership, and bought and managed properties. I've done it all, and I've been very successful moving from one business to another. I would never have been able to do all of that if all my contacts had been in one industry.

When you're working in one particular industry, of course you're going to meet a lot of other people in that same business. Sometimes it takes some planning and determination to meet people outside of your small circle. Take every opportunity your job provides to interact with people who do different things.

When I was an auditor for the IRS, my job was to audit various businesses in every possible industry. I never went in as an opponent.

On the contrary, I felt that we were in this together, to make sure the company followed the law. I always believed that was an important aspect of the work I did—to make sure they understood that I was helping them discover what was wrong and then fix it. And because of that, I developed great relationships with the people I audited.

It was a fantastic opportunity for me and a real confidence builder. To do my job properly, I had to understand how each different business operated. I went through the books and I learned so much. I could see that I could understand management and do as good or better a job in a wide variety of industries. I also was true to my word and helped the companies identify and make adjustments that kept them on the right side of the law.

Later, when I left the IRS and went into consulting for myself, many of these businesses became my first clients. They knew me, trusted me, and realized that I already had an intimate understanding of how their company operated. In turn, they often recommended me to their friends. It was important that I have a diverse client base, and I developed it quickly through personal relationships outside of my own department.

Contacts play a huge role in developing wealth. Make acquaintances inside your industry to share information and best practices; make them outside to help you learn what else is going on in the world. Doing so gives you depth to determine your decisions. Exchanging help, information, and ideas is very valuable to add to your perspective. In addition, when you have friends who are professionals and experts in other fields, their insights can only contribute to your understanding of the bigger picture.

## The Value of Contacts a Rung Above

You have colleagues in every job, people who are more or less on your professional level. But you also have clients and bosses, both of whom you may see as being on a different rung of the ladder of success. Don't be afraid to build bridges to people on other levels. For instance, if you're in school, look to your professors as well as fellow students. I had some excellent teachers, and one in particular gave me tremendous confidence: Dr. Murphy, Dean of the School of Accounting at California State University, Los Angeles. Dr. Murphy recognized my potential, helped me to apply for scholarships, and opened doors for me in the world of accounting. She was crushed when I took my degree and went to work for the IRS! (She had greater things in mind for me, but I think I did okay.) To this day, I am grateful for that relationship. Her encouragement and guidance came at a critical time in my studies.

It's hard to talk about relationships with people at a different level without talking about mentorship. The word *mentor* has come to have a lot of weight attached to it, but I've found mentors in every profession and at every level, and I've helped others up the ladder throughout my career. Rather than thinking about it in terms of "I have to find a mentor to open doors for me," think instead, "Who do I know who has done this, who can answer this question?"

Also, let me reiterate that the best way to create a great relationship with the upper management is to do a stellar job where you are. Take pride in your work. Show them you're someone worth helping to advance.

In my twenties, I worked as a window dresser. I loved the work. I would go into a window display and dress mannequins, pin garments, and work with the scenery. It's an art: the placement, what you pick, the color of the fabrics, and more. The purpose of the window displays, of course, is to motivate people to look at the window and go into the store, so as I was dressing mannequins, I was also absorbing lessons about marketing and design.

I ended up working at a department store where I met a wonderful craftsman, a longtime window trimmer who took me under his wing. When our entire department was let go, I didn't know what to do next. He told me, "You will go to Atlanta first to get more training and then go to Charlotte, North Carolina." And I did. And it changed my life. He shared not only his advice, but his contacts in the South with me. I got the training I needed to be able to find employment as a window dresser anywhere in the country, and I also jumped into a new adventure through his help. I am so grateful to have had his mentorship.

Look around wherever you are right now to see who might be in a position to help you. Your first mentor should be one who can guide you in terms of where you should seek employment and how you can go about it. Having someone who can help you evaluate your strengths and clarify what you bring to a job is invaluable. Again, this isn't some-one who can give you a job, but someone who knows the industry and knows you, and can help you see where your talents would dovetail with an employer's needs. Don't discount a mentor who, like Dr. Mur-phy, gives you encouragement and confidence, especially early in your career.

There are infinite opportunities to network with successful people and learn from them. Successful people tend to run in the same social structures, and often are leaders in professional organizations. Look around; investigate the top professional groups in your area and in your industry. It's important to put yourself in a situation where you can meet people who know more than you do, because you'll learn just by watching and listening to them.

## A Quick Caveat

You'll want to choose your friends wisely.

You can be influenced by your peers in so many ways, but one of the most important is in the use of your time. If you fall in with people who have low expectations of their own lives, you are likely to absorb that belief system. Even if you don't, your time spent with them will never be productive, your conversations never enlightening or fruitful. They may be good people, but they will not help you live the life you want to live. Time is our most precious resource and the only one we can't buy more of. You really have none to waste.

There are also people who aren't "good people." As you make new connections, it's important to judge each of them by what they do, not what kind of clothes they wear or what car they drive or anything that's external. That includes the size of their bank account. People can make money without being honorable; that doesn't mean you have to be in business with them. The questions to ask are: "Is this someone who lives with purpose? Do they make the most of their talents? What is their contribution to the world?" You want to work with people who are smart and committed and share your values.

Joining the right groups—and by this, I mean groups that are committed to helping their members move forward—can help you set the right goals. You want to be surrounded with people who have different and interesting ideas and are willing to share them, people with energy and the desire to make a difference.

Treat everyone with both respect and compassion, and be on the lookout for the kind of people—who they are on the inside—that you can rise with. Don't let anyone pull you down, and if people suggest things that are contrary to your values or don't line up with the life you want to live, just move away from them. Don't argue, don't create drama; go out and find like-minded people and spend time with them.

A related problem as you rise in the world is envy. You may find yourself with friends or family members stuck at a point in their own lives and resenting your success. Try to blunt this by including them in your circle. Mentor them; try to help them attain their own success, their own happiness. The last thing you want to do is curtail your own abilities in a misguided effort to keep them from feeling bad. Ultimately, they will choose how they wish to live their lives, either actively pursuing happiness—or not.

# Your Community

When you're building a community, first, of course, there is your family. That has always been the bedrock of my life. In a way, family is your first community in which you share your talents. And having a strong family is a contribution you make to your own community and to the larger society.

One of the lovely things about being wealthy is that you can share your blessings with others. I don't just—or even mostly—mean this in terms of money. When you're not stressed and overworked and afraid for the future, you can be open with your time and talents. Being an active leader in your community is a tremendous way to enrich your life: with relationships, with enjoyment, and with the satisfaction of giving back.

Despite my pronounced insistence on saving and paying attention to your expenses, I've never been one to hold onto money tightly. I've always wanted money to flow through me for the benefit of everyone, and I feel the same way about my knowledge, expertise, and the good that I can do. While there are several charities and universities whose work I support, I've also always been active in my community. I already mentioned the workshops I gave through a local church way back in the day, where I talked to women about financial management (and urged the cutting up of credit cards), but I also spoke at men-only retreats about finances, saving, and building for the future. Raising my kids, I was a head coach for Little League and a YMCA Indian Guide counselor. I've also looked to keep my connection with my past and honor my mother, father, and brother, all of whom have left this world, by being a strong supporter of Italian American heritage. The satisfaction of doing each of these things has been immense.

Reaching out into your community and giving your time, talent, and passion is a way to be a leader, develop contacts, and live a rich and full life. I also believe that by strengthening our communities, we help build stronger foundations for our own businesses. I'm in real estate; a strong community only helps the real estate market, making it a more desirable place for people to live and work. This is just one of the many ways in which doing good helps you to do well.

## RECAP: RELATIONSHIPS

- **Go out and meet people.** Make acquaintances in all walks of life. Everyone has something to offer.

- **Network within your own industry.** Sharing information, resources, and advice is a critical component of building wealth.

- **Look for the people who need you and your business.** Make friends with people who might become clients.

- **Meet people and learn about industries outside of your own.**

- **Don't be afraid to develop relationships with people a rung above you.** Professors and bosses can become mentors and partners.

- **Don't hoard either your money or your talents.** Look for ways to be an active member, even a leader, in your community. Do good to do well.

# CHAPTER FOUR

## CLARIFYING YOUR VISION

One of the most important things I learned as a child was the kind of life I wanted to live. I was always happiest when I was working, and that's largely because I chose work that I enjoyed. When it stopped being fun, or when I found something to do that was more fun (and I have to tell you, hunting for lost golf balls and reselling them was a lot more fun than carting around a heavy bag of clubs), I changed direction. I was lucky in that I was always clear about the life I wanted to lead, even if I didn't yet know the kind of work I wanted to do.

Knowing what you want out of life provides a True North to guide you when you have decisions to make. And you will have decisions to make every single day. I can't overstate the importance of knowing what you want—that is, if you want to get it.

## Have a Goal

You picked up this book in pursuit of a goal. Given the title of the book, I'm going to say your goal was creating wealth. I'm all in favor of that, but you're also going to need to be a little more specific.

I don't find it useful to think of success in specific dollar amounts. There have been times in my life when I was making plenty of money, but I wasn't happy and my family wasn't happy. I'll give you the full story when I talk about mistakes, but briefly, I was in a job that ate up all my time. For almost two years, I was absent from the lives of my children and my wife. That was not the life I wanted to live.

What about you?

Think about what really matters to you. Do you want to work flat out for three months of the year, like my father, or are you only happy when you're building on your most recent success, like my mother? Do you have a family? Are you pursuing an art or writing a book or creating a movement? You have to know what you really want to have any chance of getting it.

What is your goal? Take a minute and write it down. Wanting money for the sake of a number in the bank is not a great goal. When my wife and I hit a million dollars in annual revenue, we barely noticed it. I'm not kidding. I didn't realize it myself until one day, I was doing the books and there it was, in black and white. Bernice and I were working together out of our home, and I ran into the next room and told her. Her first reaction was worry that we'd spoil the kids! The thing is—it didn't change our lives on a day-to-day basis at all. I splurged on a new car, my first Jaguar. It was the symbol for me that we'd succeeded. Quick story: When I was just starting out in life and became old enough to drive, I drove an old clunker; if a girl I was dating didn't like my car, I found another girl. So for me, driving a Jaguar was a tremendous mark of achievement. Other than that, nothing changed. Making a million a year was a side product of doing work we enjoyed, work we shared first as a couple, then as a family.

Now, Bernice would have been happy to stop at a million. She felt all our needs were met, and she would have been content to take things a little easier and just keep managing what we already had. But I genuinely like to keep busy. I'm never happier than when I'm working. Even when I read, it's mostly to learn something; what they call "beach reads" I do not find relaxing. I hate to waste time. My daughter Ann remembers me "in perpetual motion," a human dynamo. I won't deny it.

For me, the freedom of being my own boss was always the ultimate goal, plus the fact that along the way I was doing what I loved with the people I loved. It's been a great life, and I'm forever grateful to Bernice for understanding that my happiness came from *doing*, not having.

Wealth, to me, is about freedom. When you think of your goal, think instead about what that number in the bank buys you. It bought my dad nine months of the year to read good books, cook great meals, and spend time with his family. It can buy you the opportunity to travel the world or make a difference in your community or say no to work you dislike. I want you to focus on the math every step of the way, but you need to understand that money is the means to an end. The end is always freedom—but what that freedom will do for you is an individual choice.

Knowing your goal can motivate you when things are down. There are always going to be times when you're tired or discouraged or you need to walk away from a situation that didn't work out. Those are hard moments. But remembering your goal and what that freedom will bring you can keep you from giving up. And giving up is the only real mistake you can make.

I always wanted to have the freedom to be able to walk away from a bad situation, and I always had that, even when money was tight. It's a mindset just as much as it is dollars in the bank. Not that money in the bank isn't important, but that's not what comes first. First comes understanding that you are not stuck, that you have options. You have strengths.

## Know Thyself

It's great to know where you want to go in life, but it's equally import-ant to figure out how you're going to get there, and the key to that is taking a good hard look at where you are now. Lots of people love to plan and outline and set goals, but the thing they often forget to do is take the time to figure out where they are right now. Where are you starting from?

A map is no good if you don't know where you already are.

You have some skills, but you also have some weaknesses. This is the time to figure out which is which. For instance, let's say you're good at computers. That could be a terrific skill, depending on what you want to do. Being able to program in several languages can be very useful if you want to get into software design, but it's not going to help you as much if your goal is to train race horses or start a home painting business.

Remember when I went to work for General Electric and the guy next to me was making twice the money because he had a college degree? I realized that education was a real weakness for me *at that moment in my life*. I didn't do well in high school until I started to study things I enjoyed, like my business classes—and, to be fair, once I started seeing the practical applications of things I hadn't much enjoyed, like algebra. Realizing that a college degree was a missing piece for me and deciding that I was going to take that on were big moments for me. Since then, I've been on a path of continual learning. Taking action turned a weakness into a strength. That's what I want you to understand: A weakness isn't a fatal flaw, it's not some insurmountable destiny, it's just something you have to address if you want to succeed.

Be honest with yourself. What skills do you already have, will they help you get where you want to go, and where do you need to improve? Communication skills, interpersonal skills, fund-raising skills, field-specific knowledge—all of these things matter. Now take a look at things in your life at this moment in time that need improvement.

Something is only a weakness if it interferes with the life you want. My dad didn't like to work hard, and nine months out of the year, he didn't. But those other three months, he worked nonstop. This was how he chose to live his life, and while it would drive me crazy, it worked for him. He was a success because he did what he had to do to have the life he wanted.

Take stock. What is the life you want and what do you have to do to be in a position to get it?

I'm not going to strand you here. I have some ideas of foundational things you need, and I go into them in depth in the next chapter. In fact, I've already given you some hints: You need people to work with, to learn from, and to pay you. You need money to invest, and for that you need savings, and for that you need a budget. I'll give you another one, an important one: You need to be good at something. Mastery can be leveraged.

But I want you to look beyond anything I can suggest. I don't know your particular field; I don't know what exact skills will be helpful to you. Look around you—who is succeeding? What skills/attributes/accomplishments do they have that you don't have? Maybe they work longer hours, maybe they specialize in something, maybe they're risk-takers, maybe they have a variety of certificates in technical areas that are useful in your profession. If you rely too much on my list of (admittedly important) attributes, you'll miss out on the things that will make a difference in your life that I know nothing about. Being creative, thinking outside the box—that's another foundational skill. Practice it now by coming up with a list of the things that can propel you forward and a second list of the things that are holding you back.

This isn't just important for when you start your own business. This self-knowledge can help you stand out from the crowd when you are looking for a job. When you go to an interview, be able to explain what you can offer. Use a professional résumé that accurately reflects your training and abilities, but be able to talk about the intangibles as well. Being able to fruitfully discuss how you can be of value and mesh with the company can create a relationship even if you don't get that particular job. Someone well-impressed will remember you for an even better position down the road.

## What Are Your Values?

It's also important for you to know who you are in the world. What are your values? What do you stand for? There are some things that are non-negotiable for you; maybe it's how you believe people should be treated, your religious values, or your business ethics. Trust that they will be tested someday and you'll need to decide if you're really willing to live your principles.

When I graduated from college with a bachelor's degree in accounting, I went to work for the IRS. But not right away. First, I went to work for a local CPA firm. They wanted me—expected me—to keep the books in a way that was very different from the one I'd been taught in college. I lasted two weeks. I had a choice, and I chose to live up to my own values, my own integrity. I never regretted the decision to leave, even though at that moment, I didn't have another job lined up. I soon started working for the IRS, and the rest is history.

I don't take bribes. I keep my word. I live an ethical life. I have found it impossible to work or even have friendly relationships with people who don't share these basic values. And I don't know who said "Nice guys finish last," because I have never found that to be true. My integrity has opened more doors for me than I could have imagined, and it has allowed me to work again and again with top people because they know they can trust what I say. Integrity is a rare currency in the world, and I urge you not to squander yours.

# Leverage Your Day Job

Once again, I'm going to start with the least glamorous part of building wealth: the day job. Having a paycheck coming in for as long as possible is critical to supporting yourself and building your investment funds. But a day job can offer a lot more than that. It can provide a place to learn the skills you need to build your own business, all on someone else's dime.

Just as you took stock of your own strengths and weaknesses, take a good long look at your day job. First, look at the job itself. Is it challenging you? Is it teaching you skills and providing experience and contacts in an industry that will support your wealth-building? Here's what I mean by that: Are you getting a chance to read contracts? To learn about the industry? To meet people who are making things happen in their field? Do you get to see the books? A day job moving boxes in a warehouse might support your family, but it's not going to support your future. Working in different areas will teach you skills you can transfer to any business.

If you have a job that's not going to help you get where you want to go, start looking for a new job. Really. I've walked away from most of my day jobs at one time or another, usually because for whatever reason I could no longer move forward in them. You have to be strategic.

Once you decide your day job is helping you move forward, then you need to determine how you can make the most of it. I am a big believer in squeezing every possible asset out of a situation. It goes without saying that you're going to work harder than others, but don't just work hard, work smart. Look to see what the people in the other departments are doing. What can you learn from them? Can you take on some extra responsibilities for your boss or supervisor that will help you learn another part of the business? How can you meet people higher up or at other companies as a peer? How can you learn more or gain insight into not only your company, but your entire field?

Set short-term goals for yourself and meet them. Take advantage of every opportunity. This might mean working late, volunteering for extra duties, and showing up at every optional lecture or get-together. Be creative in your suggestions and thorough in your work; do more than is expected. You're putting the time in now to hone your skills in your industry and meet people as a go-getter.

Remember to make the most of your company's relationships in the outside world as well. When I worked for the IRS and later the state government, I audited a lot of companies. I was always fair; it was important to me to sit down with everyone as a peer. I wasn't the enemy; together, we were going to fix what needed to be fixed to comply with the law. The relationship I created, even under what is normally seen as difficult circumstances, was always one of mutual respect. When I left government work, some of those same people hired me as a consultant. Not because I'd shown them preferential treatment, but because I'd treated them with integrity, fairness, and competence. Build relationships on that foundation, and you'll always have people who want to work with you, whether you're in business for someone else or for yourself.

## Risk Tolerance

Most people think of "risk tolerance" in terms of how much someone is willing to gamble on a new stock or even at a casino. But as you can see from my story with the dealership, sometimes you have to be willing to risk your best ideas; your hard work; your blood, sweat, and tears. If you're not willing to put everything into a project, then don't do it. Look for something else. If you're only half committed, you'll do a lousy job, and you'll always be looking for when it's time to bolt. That is not the pathway to success.

Knowing your risk tolerance and under what circumstances it fluctuates can help you decide where to put your focus.

Because here's the thing about risk tolerance: It's not absolute. I've done a lot of things that, from the outside, looked pretty risky. I've sued quite a few people, and I've been sued many times. I've left jobs on a matter of principle or just because I was getting bored—well-paying jobs—with a family to support, and with nothing else lined up ahead of time. Someone looking at me would say, wow, here's a guy who takes crazy risks.

Nothing could be less true.

Let's take employment first. I can't imagine anything more detrimental to your wealth than staying in a situation where you weren't using your talents, where there was no outlet for your ambitions, or where you weren't getting the respect and financial rewards that were promised and that you deserved. None of these are situations in which you would do your best work or move ahead, plus you'd probably be miserable. I know I would have been if I'd stayed in any of these situations. The risk of leaving was balanced out by the opportunity cost of staying.

Plus, it was never that much of a risk. Risk tolerance is to a large extent about perception. It used to be that if you lived in a small town with, say, one big factory, your options were pretty limited. You worked for them or for the people who worked for them, or you scrambled. And if the factory moved, the economy of the entire town went bust. But that was never my situation and it's probably not yours. I worked for most of my life in or near big cities. There were always new opportunities, and when there weren't, I moved to another state. Today, with the mobility we have (not to mention the opportunities to work virtually), even people in one-industry towns have options.

More important than the number and kinds of jobs available, however, was my perception of my ability to find a job. I never doubted it. I wouldn't even tell Bernice when I'd quit because I knew I'd find something else so quickly, it wasn't going to matter. She didn't need to start economizing because a new paycheck was going to be coming in before she realized the old paycheck had stopped. It was never an issue.

How could I be so sure? First of all, I was confident in my basic skills. I knew I had a lot to offer and would work hard; I would be an asset to any employer. And with the number and breadth of relationships I had, I only had to put the word out that I was available and people would start looking for ways to work with me. This isn't bragging. It was a direct result of the amount of time and energy I spent developing my skills, helping my friends and my community, and making the most of my nature and work ethic.

You only perceive it as a risk if you perceive that you might fail.

Let's take that idea and look at real estate. I poured our entire savings into buying rental properties time after time. Was it ever a sure thing that I would make money on those properties? No. There have been properties I bought that I had to walk away from, and I'll give you details of those in Chapter Eight.

But from my perspective, buying a property I then had to sell was not a failure. It was a learning experience. My parents went bankrupt not once, but twice. Each time, we bounced back. When I graduated from college and went to work for the IRS at a very nice salary, my mother, with her third-grade education, was still making more money than I was. To the end of his days, my dad lived exactly the life he wanted to live. A failed business, a bad purchase, a lawsuit— none of those things had any lasting impact on my family's happiness. Growing up, I learned that there was nothing there to fear.

I'm not saying go out and make a bad purchase. On the contrary, in Chapter Eight, I tell you all the things you should look for and stay away from. I want to set you up for success. But I'm also not too worried if you fail a few times. If you're too risk-averse to try, you'll never succeed.

# Partnerships

I've had a lot of partners. Mostly, I've discovered that I prefer to work on my own and call my own shots, but that doesn't mean that partners haven't been critical to my success over the years.

Let me start with the story of a partnership that never happened. You see, there was this girl . . . .

You may have started to grin, and that's fine, but don't let it distract you from the fact that too many people marry the wrong person, or for the wrong reason. And many more find themselves at that crossroads, as I did. There was a girl in North Carolina who I liked very much. We went out dancing together. She was pretty, she was funny, and we always had a great time. But she wanted to get married and start a family right away. I told her I wasn't ready to get married; I worked days and was going to college part-time. I wanted to get my degree so I could advance in the world. But she waved that off. I could go to work, she told me, for her father. There wasn't any reason in the world we couldn't get married right away.

But there was. The biggest reason we couldn't, shouldn't, get married was that she didn't share my vision for my life. And equally, I didn't share her vision for her life. Working for her father would have been a great future for a lot of young men, but it wasn't what I wanted to do.

Recognizing when a partner has a different vision—whether it's a life partner or a business partner, or both—is critically important.

I broke up with the girl and moved to California to be closer to my dad. When I met Bernice, the woman I would marry, she instantly understood how important a college degree was to me. Rather than try to talk me out of it, she started thinking of how she could support me in what I wanted to do—and she ended up supporting both of us financially while I went back to school full-time. Bernice never tried to talk me out of my dreams. She was sometimes the voice of cold, hard facts—I heard "You don't have the money for that building" more than once—but when I told her I'd find a way, she never doubted me. More importantly, she never made me doubt myself.

This is what you want in any partnership. You want someone who brings skills to the table, whether it's a strength in an area you don't have, relationships that will smooth your way, or the ability to bring out the best in you. You don't want someone who's going to make your life more difficult. As I mentioned earlier, I had a partner whose wife would give him a list of criticisms and "suggestions" every Monday for me to implement, and he would hand them to me and expect them to get done. I was his partner, not his lackey. Ours was not a relationship that lasted.

In that same vein, make sure you value your partners and their contributions. I always wanted the best for everyone. Life isn't a zero-sum game—for you to win, someone else has to lose. We're all in this together. And if a partner doesn't value you, then it's also time to move on. I was in business with someone where the partnership was fifty-fifty in everything—except where it mattered, in a contract. Here's what happened. A friend and I decided to start a car leasing company. He already had a dealership, and I had worked for him and knew how to run a business. He provided the financing and I provided the expertise and management. It was an immediate and ongoing success, but he never did make me a partner. He valued what I did, but not enough to keep his word.

Ultimately, when the promised partnership didn't materialize, I had to leave, but we remained friends. He recommended me for jobs and always spoke highly of me. On my end, I will always value what I learned from him. He was a smart man who knew his business extremely well and was willing to teach me every aspect of it; to this day, I consider him a mentor. Not valuing his contribution to my life would be dishonest. It also wouldn't serve me. If you can, don't ever be bitter. Look for the positive in every relationship—even the ones you have to walk away from. There isn't enough time and energy to waste on disparaging the past.

If you can, try to start out partnering with someone new in a small way, on a single project. You can't always do this; sometimes you have to go all in on something to know if it's going to work. With the dealership, I had to show I could make the lease business profitable. I brought to the table an outsider's way of thinking and I wasn't afraid to try new ideas. My mentor had my back the entire way. I built an amazingly successful business, and I would never have succeeded if I hadn't completely committed to it. You can't always guarantee how a business relationship will turn out, but you can make sure that when you walk away, you have no regrets about how you behaved.

# Write Your Own Story

Speaking of having no regrets . . . you remember my brother, Henry, and how at the end of his life, his deepest regret was that he hadn't done more with his talents?

Now, I don't think Henry regretted not having more money to leave behind or that he'd wanted to run an empire or live on a yacht. But I do think he regretted not helping people by sharing his knowledge and expertise, not building on the opportunities he'd been given. I don't want you to have those same regrets.

Sometimes we get carried along by the tide of life because we don't know what we want or we don't want to make decisions that might be difficult. Those are the very decisions you have to make. You've spent some time now clarifying your goals and seeing where you need to build to have the foundations for success. But you can clarify and plan until the cows come home; until you make a decision, until you act, you will never have more than you do right this very minute. You will never do more with your life than you already have.

If that were to happen to you, what would you regret?

I'll tell you about a decision I made. It's the one where I decided to leave my life in North Carolina and move out to California to be with my dad. There were a lot of things going on, and I was at a fork in my life. I could have stayed in the South, married the girl, gone to work for her dad, and lived a very simple, safe life. That's where my friends were, where my job was, and where a life of "good enough" beckoned me.

I made the decision to leave all of that and move across the country.

It's not that staying would not have been a decision—it's that it wouldn't have *felt like* a decision. That's the danger. The danger is not in choosing that this is what you want, it's in letting it sneak up on you because you don't want to choose. You don't want to decide. You don't want to write your own story.

I actively chose a different life. Part of it was that when my brother called and told me that family was the most important thing and that Dad needed me, I agreed with him. In my heart, that is what I will always believe—that family matters more than anything. And so I decided to live my values and go to California.

But I also decided that a "good enough" life wasn't good enough for me. That was an active decision, and it came at a cost. I left a lot of things behind. But I needed to, because I wanted something more. I wanted to write a different story of my life.

You need to write your own story. There are a lot of people who don't want you to change because change would upset their own apple cart. If you're a great assistant, why would your boss want you to apply to a better job in a different department? Who would keep their calendar if you went to law school? Your friends might try to talk you out of moving to Maine because they're not ever moving from the same block where they were born. But you can't live their story—at least not without a lifetime of regrets.

Take your chance. Make your mistakes. Learn from them; don't retreat in defeat. Make decisions. It's your life. Write your own story.

## CASE STUDY

## Turning Around a Credit Union

I want to give you the full story of my time with a local credit union, one that was facing immense challenges. In point of fact, the credit union was in real trouble, which is why they needed me. When I came on board, the credit union was facing a staggering default rate on their loans. Twenty-five percent of borrowers were delinquent on their loans—one in four. Take a minute to let that sink in. Now, a credit union is dependent on membership from the community, and in turn, it is meant to serve its community. But no institution can thrive—or even survive for long—with that level of delinquency.

First, how I landed that job was a perfect example of the power of relationships. When I was working as an examiner for the State of California, I worked very closely with a number of credit unions. I also had a good reputation among my colleagues, so when a friend and fellow examiner left to go run some credit unions, he remembered me. He knew of my expertise and that I already had a good deal of experience within the credit union business as an examiner, and when someone reached out to him, he recommended me. This is how it's done. You do stellar work, you maintain your professional relationships, and you get remembered and recommended. And it wasn't just him. When I met with the credit union board, they had already checked my references, which included several people in their industry. I was given glowing recommendations not just for my fairness and character, but for my vision, particularly in terms of developing new business. It really was a match made in heaven: I was the man they needed, and for me, the timing was right. I was burned out from working for the state and was eager for a new challenge. I just didn't realize how big a challenge it would prove to be.

My initial goal was simple: clear up the delinquency problem. Unfortunately, it wasn't until I interviewed with the board that I saw the books and realized how enormous the problem was—and yes, I did wonder for a minute what I had gotten myself into. But tackling the delinquency rate fell squarely into my skill set. First of all, it was a perfect example of working to make both sides happy. The credit union would be happy because they would no longer have a crippling delinquency rate, and the customers would be happy because they would no longer be struggling with loans they clearly could not repay. These were community members, and they were getting those loans to build businesses and homes that would only make the community stronger. Getting rid of that level of stress would be an all-around win for the credit union, the individual, and the community at large.

But there was another community here, and that is the department I inherited when I took the job. By and large, these were the people who had gotten the credit union into the spot it was in to begin with by making ill-advised loans. It was also overstaffed, a point I'll come back to later. But I never start by firing everyone; that's counterproductive. You have to develop relationships, see who maybe needs training or better direction, see who wants to work, who wants to learn. But I did let them know that things were changing, and the first thing I did was review the paperwork they filled out when considering a loan application.

Right away, I could see that the application was inadequate. It was not extensive enough to make loans. I redesigned it immediately and then continued to fine-tune it to be more efficient, but I gave my team something they could use that would help them to turn down bad loans.

The credit union was church-based, which meant that the community it served—and the people who were delinquent—were all members of Baptist churches up and down the state. Some of them were even pastors.

How do you talk to a pastor about being behind on their loan? The same way I talked to everybody else, as it turns out. I was firm, but I was also very much on their side. They had gotten into a difficult situation and they needed to be able to see a way out.

Here's how I did it. I sat down with the books and I called every single delinquent member, more than one hundred of them. I talked, I listened, and I made them see that I was an ally, not an enemy. I would take care of their financing on a new, restructured payment schedule; it was very important that the payments would be something they could really live with. To sweeten the deal, I marked every loan as current under the new structure, even if it had been (as some were) as much as six months in arrears. I helped people clean up their credit and I created personal relationships as well as plans they could succeed in repaying. Within three months, I had brought the delinquency rate down from 25 percent to 3 percent. And if anyone missed a payment on the restructured deal, I called them personally to find out why. It was immensely successful for the credit union, but it only worked because I wanted to make both sides, both the credit union and the borrower, happy.

The next thing I did was make sure the federal government would guarantee our deposits. FDIC insurance wasn't something the credit union offered when I went to work for them, and although the paperwork was a hassle, it was without question the right thing to do. Now, if there was a loss or if the credit union went under, people wouldn't lose the money they had entrusted to us. This is where vision starts to come in. You shouldn't see any business, even in finance, as being just about making money. We had a moral obligation to protect our clients.

I also had a vision to develop new business. When I came in, the credit union had assets of $850,000. Clearly, there was room to grow. My next step was to develop a relationship with the bank. What I wanted was virtually unheard of at the time: I wanted to develop a process by which our credit union members could write checks on their accounts. And I did, with the help of the bank; they serviced our checks with their own. As the in-between entity, it was advantageous for them because they kept our money overnight as they processed the checks; our checks strengthened their books. And the win for us was being able to offer check-writing services to credit union members. Once that was in place, you could hardly tell the difference between our credit union and the bank down the street.

The next thing I did was reach out to the national credit union to borrow money. We had money from our members, but the national credit union offered funding based on our dividends. Suddenly, we were awash with outside funding and I was actively looking to make loans. I developed equity loans or second-trust deed loans, and suddenly the portfolio of the credit union was ratcheting up.

Here's the important part: All of this new business, which created new streams of income for the credit union, was putting my own people to work. Remember I told you I'd revisit the idea that we'd been overstaffed? Suddenly, everyone was working. I didn't need to let anyone go because now with the new loans and expanded portfolio, there was more than enough to do. Our expenses didn't go up even as income increased because I trained my staff to be more efficient even as I offered new challenges, and so I didn't have to lay anyone off. Your vision can't be just for yourself.

But I still wasn't done. We now had a strong portfolio, national money to lend to our local communities, a low delinquency rate, and a well-trained and efficient staff. Now was the time to start reaching out, and I developed a plan to lend money to the churches themselves. Churches are always in need of repair. They need a new roof, a new hall, a paint job. Improving the church makes it more appealing to churchgoers, and even the act of having a church drive helps to create a strong community as everyone pitches in to help.

The question was, where would the credit union get enough money to make so many extremely large loans? Again, it was about reaching out to the community we served. I would go to the church meetings and tell the leadership that we would be happy to make the loans, but on the condition that they and their flock join the credit union and use it as their bank. Entire congregations joined the credit union. I built the assets of our credit union from $850,000 to over $15 million in the space of three years.

How did I do all this? It was a tremendous combination of relationships (some I had, most I worked to build), experience, vision, negotiation, and caring. Having audited credit unions for years, I was able to take the best practices of several of them and put them to use in ours.

What I want you to learn from this is how you can really make something out of nothing, out of less than nothing. They were in a real bind at the credit union when I came in; nothing about what I did was easy. I was on the phone, calling people at 6:30 in the morning (something one is no longer allowed to do, I might add) to restructure their loans. I was going out evenings and weekends to meet with church congregations and leadership. I had to stretch myself and think outside the established norms for how business was done; instead, I had to think, why not? Why not issue checks? Why not build partnerships with the churches? It was time-consuming and at times extremely difficult, but it was also exhilarating to see the difference I was able to make.

Anyone can come into a managerial position and just keep the ball rolling. But you can have a tremendous impact by using creativity, focus, and all your expertise and people skills in a challenging situation. The key is to take ownership—of the challenges, of the people you serve, and of your own career. Your success is in your hands.

## RECAP: CLARIFYING YOUR VISION

- **Know what your goal is.** Hint: It's not a number in the bank. It's what that number will make possible in your life.

- **Acknowledge both your strengths and your weaknesses.** Remember that a weakness isn't permanent; you can get better at math, meet new people, understand your industry. Focus on shoring up what you need to get to the next step.

- **Leverage your day job.** Be relentless about making sure you are learning everything and meeting everyone you can from the situation.

- **Understand your own tolerance for risk.** Remember that risk is largely a matter of perception. Work to minimize the risk, but also remember the opportunity cost of not taking action.

- **Look for people who share both your values and your vision.**

- **Don't be afraid to make decisions that will lead to the life you want to live.** Don't listen to people who want to hold you back. Write your own story.

# CHAPTER FIVE

## MASTERY

You've reached a certain level of expertise in your job, in developing business relationships, in your particular niche. You have some money to invest as well as time to manage a new endeavor. You have reached a stage of mastery.

Now what do you do?

## Your Path to Success

It may be that you picked up this book hoping to get some simple "invest all your money here while hustling at that side gig there" advice. If that's what you wanted, let me suggest you run out and buy a lottery ticket. You have as much chance of getting rich with that advice as with the lottery. Why?

Because everyone is unique.

I got wealthy in the specific way that I did because of the specific skills I brought to my life. I also got lucky. I've been lucky in love not once, but twice, each time finding a life partner who shared my values and my commitment. I was lucky to have parents who taught me about business and life, and lucky to find along the way the specific mentors who could help me on my path. And I used my personal strengths to build on every lucky break.

You will do the same.

Not that you will follow the same path, but you will follow the same signposts. That's what I want this book to do for you: lay out what tools you need, what mindset will help you, what relationships you need to develop and how you can best do that. But all of the things I'm talking about, even when I go into detail in Chapter Eight on how to invest in real estate, everything I say should be used in the service of your own strengths. It has to be. If I were going to write a book that could only help those with my exact skill set, it would be for an audience of two, maybe three individuals. I want to help a lot more people than that.

I want to help *you*.

Here are the foundational things you need to be able to do to build wealth:

- Read a contract.
- Understand the math.
- Develop relationships.
- Negotiate so that everyone wins.
- Leverage your strengths.

You may need to work on some of these things to get them to the level required. You don't have to go back to college to become an accountant, a lawyer, or a doctor, but you do need to understand what your income versus outgo will be. If you buy an apartment complex that needs to be 100 percent occupied for you to break even, that is a recipe for failure. Numbers are your friends. Understand them, work with them, and they will be very, very faithful to you.

Ignore them at your peril.

One quick aside about numbers. Some people think they can get away with not understanding the math because they have a partner, business manager, or agent who does. I can't stress enough that putting that much power into someone else's hands is a bad career decision. Not only are you giving away the keys to your financial kingdom, but you're also vastly curtailing your ability to make good financial decisions because you don't want to put in the work to understand the math.

Let me give you an example. I helped put together a deal for a restaurant that included the land it sat on. I became a partner with two other entrepreneurs and what they offered me was a partnership in the restaurant itself. But I looked at the numbers and I knew the real money was in the land. I chose to partner in the land deal only, and let them split the restaurant 50/50 between them. I made the best possible deal for myself—and created the ability to walk away when it no longer made sense for me to stay—because I understood a profit/loss sheet, the risks of the restaurant business, and the value of real estate. That is true freedom.

If you are a math-phobe, decide right now that you will overcome it. Do whatever you have to do. You will be relieving yourself of a tremendous shortcoming once you can look at and understand what a deal does (and does not) do for you financially.

The same goes for being able to read and understand a contract. This is where choosing the right day job can be extremely useful. If you work for someone who reads a lot of contracts, then you should read them, too. Ask questions. Learn what makes a good deal and what's a deal breaker. Understand how specific language will be interpreted in court. Expect that someday you will be sued, or that you will want to sue someone else. Knowing ahead of time whether or not you have a case is very valuable, as is understanding the full ramifications of a contract before you bind yourself with a signature.

This is not the glamorous stuff. This is not the jet-setting, Monte Carlo lifestyle. But this is how you get rich—and make sure you keep the money you've worked so hard to earn.

# Contracts

Let me reiterate some key advice here: Read a lot of contracts. I can't tell you how many people rely on a lawyer or an agent or a business adviser to tell them whether or not they should sign a contract. This is a recipe for disaster. If you're going to be an expert in nothing else, become an expert in the kinds of contracts to which you will be binding yourself.

So how can you read a lot of contracts?

I started reading real estate contracts with my mother. She understood the terms and she really understood the money, but she didn't always catch the fine print. And I saw how her other "partners" took advantage of those clauses whenever they could.

So my first non-negotiable piece of advice to you is this: If there's anything in the contract that you don't understand—a clause, a paragraph, even a sentence—it is worth every penny to hire someone to explain it to you. Do not sign something you don't understand. And take every contract offered to you as an opportunity to learn about how they're written.

But rather than start with contracts where you have something on the line, why not start with contracts where you don't? When I got started leasing cars, I spent the weekend going to other car dealerships and looking into their leases. They would offer me a contract and I would go home and dissect it. I'd compare it to the other contracts from the other dealerships. I could see what made sense and what was a lot of nonsense designed to protect them from every possible eventuality. When I crafted my own contract for car leases, it was pages shorter than my competitors' contracts and far easier for my clients to read and understand, giving me an immediate edge.

Right now, you probably work for someone else who likely has contracts with vendors, clients, etc. Is there a way you can be useful to your employer while at the same time educating yourself on the kinds of contracts they see? You can find templates for all kinds of contracts online; take a look, see what's standard and what's not. See what business classes are offered near you and make friends with the professors and fellow students. Learn from each other. Read and make notes on every contract you can get your hands on and do what you need to do to understand the terms.

You don't just want to understand what kinds of clauses need to be taken out; you also want to know what you need to add in to protect yourself. A lot of people will try to talk you out of adding things into the contract. "Barbera," my real estate broker would say to me, "there's no point adding this into the contract, they'll never agree to it." Stick to your guns. I insisted on adding several clauses and they nearly always agreed to them—sometimes without discussion. Now, my real estate broker adds my clauses into all of his contracts for his other clients. Why? Not because they're unfair or stack the deck, but because they're reasonable and they spell out what our understanding is.

A good contract should clearly state everyone's responsibilities and expectations, and should provide clarity about what will happen if something goes wrong. When I take someone to court, it's because they did not fulfill their responsibilities, and I had it in writing that they would. Should they have signed something that specified they would do such-and-such, or which guaranteed that what they presented to me was accurate, if they wouldn't or it wasn't? No. I always act in good faith and they should have as well. Just as you should. Be straightforward, put in clauses that protect you, and then be prepared to enforce them. Understanding the contract inside and out puts you in a position of strength.

## Do the Math

I have already mentioned how important it is to understand the numbers yourself. Let me repeat: Do not abdicate the responsibility of your financial success to anyone else. Take accounting classes, develop a family budget, learn to read a profit/loss statement. Get comfortable with the kinds of numbers you'll see and make sure you understand what they mean.

Once you have a basic familiarity with what the real numbers of your life are, then you can see how changing the numbers impacts you. For instance, I've already talked about the importance of living below your income. It's hard to convince people to put their money into your projects if you don't have any kind of track record, which is why you need money to invest in yourself. You need to be building up your savings, and this is where changing some numbers can have a real impact. Getting a smaller apartment, bringing in a roommate, getting a part-time job—these are all about shifting numbers so that more money comes in than goes out. And while eating in, driving an older car, and going to the park instead of having a gym membership won't move the needle as quickly, they are the kinds of choices that will add up over the long run.

You need to run your financial life deliberately. Most people spend the money they have, maybe putting some away for the future and maybe not. You're not just putting away for the distant future—you're putting away for tomorrow as well. Because tomorrow, you will need that money to buy a business, invest in your education, or buy your first rental property. I like to think of this as dynamic savings. You're going to use that money sooner rather than later, but the investment you make with these savings will fuel the rest of your life.

Very early on, I started trading on the stock market. I won some, I lost some, but I learned every step of the way what to look for, how not to follow the crowd. It is up to you to learn about the stock market, and beyond the scope of this book to teach you. You need to read, to ask questions, to follow your own instinct about which companies are poised to provide real value.

I will say that day trading was one of the more exciting facets of my very early career. Every day, I would make trades before going to work. It was exhilarating. And then the market dropped, I had a margin call, and the broker sold the stock. I lost a lot of money that day.

So maybe stay away from day trading.

It was a terrific education, however. The energy of it got me hooked on the potential of the stock market, and once I understood that this wasn't going to be a get-rich-quick scheme, I started to become savvier in my investments. I made the biggest shift in my view of finances, one I urge you to make right now, when I started looking at long-term investment horizons. I keep a varied portfolio and I liquidated it many times in order to have the funds to purchase a property I wanted. Once the deal had gone through and the cash flow was positive once more, back into the market I went, always looking for long-term value.

Don't be afraid of the stock market. I never invested more than I could afford to lose and I never—after my day trading stint—invested for the quick money. I understood that the stock market was one pathway to wealth, and studying it from the outside or on some theoretical level would never have taught me half as much as actually investing in it. I needed to have something real on the line.

There was a time when I was on a local college board and I helped them with their investments. I grew their funds greatly over a period of several years. And then I told them it was time to take it out of the stock market. I felt that stocks in general were overvalued. I can't claim to have guessed how far the market would go down at the time, but I knew that downward was the direction it was heading. I recommended selling all stocks and putting the money in safer waters for the time being.

They refused.

This continues to mystify me, because I was the expert they had entrusted for years with their money. They had always agreed with my recommendations because that was my role on the board—to be their money guy. Not a single other person brought real-world experience to investing. But the minute I suggested they sell, it was as if I became the enemy.

I think the problem was twofold. First, it wasn't really their money. They were stewards of it, but it wasn't theirs. It wasn't their savings on the line. This is the difference you'll find in terms of passion and understanding when you risk some of your own money in any investment.

Just as an aside, I believe this is true of older college students as well. Going to college, or back to college, when you're older is more of a risk than just sliding into it out of high school. You are sacrificing more to get there, and so you are likely to do better and get more from the experience. That was certainly true for me. In almost every situation, having something real on the line will lead to you working harder, being more open to advice, and getting more out of the situation.

Back to the board and their lack of financial acumen. Remember I talked about how some things feel like you're not really making a decision—you're just "letting things ride"? I think that also played a part in their (disastrous) choice not to follow my recommendation. It is always easier to make a decision by not making one than by actively choosing. No one on that board did their own independent research or put any effort at all into understanding—or even into rebutting—

my argument. They simply didn't want to make a decision to pull the money and then miss out if the market went up. They didn't want to be wrong, and it felt safer to do nothing than to take action.

This is where numbers could have saved them. Understanding what the real cost of missing out on the market going up another few points meant when stacked against the risk of it falling—even just understanding the math behind the investments they had (up until that point) placed in my hands—would have saved them a lot of grief.

Don't be a sheep. Learn—actively learn—about the numbers that impact your investments, your business, and your life. Numbers will help you make better decisions, minimize risk, and maximize profit.

# Develop Relationships

I've already talked about the value of building relationships. Here, I'm going to ask you to look at your goals, look at how you plan to reach them, and start deliberately building the relationships that will help you succeed.

But first, I want to say something about people.

Relationships are about the nuances between people. When you understand those nuances, you are better able to meet everyone's needs, work together, and create great situations for yourself, your community, and your family. You don't just build relationships to help you forward your business concerns or even just to build a better community or a better world. Part of the reason you need to focus on relationships with other people is that you need experience understanding those nuances. You need to learn about people, and you especially need to learn to recognize the best people—smart, honest, hardworking people. Because those are the ones you want to be in business with.

When I worked for the IRS, I always made sure to have lunch with the people I was auditing. It wasn't just because I wanted to create a cooperative relationship—I always took the position that we were working together to make sure the laws were met, not that I was out to "catch" them—but because I could tell everything I needed to know after ten minutes of talking to them in a relaxed environment.

Once people relax, they tell you who they are in every interaction, with every aside or pointed comment. Even the way they treated the waitstaff would reveal something. I got good at reading those nuances, and pretty soon I knew what I would find when I looked through their books just by eating a meal with them.

You're not going to like everyone you meet, and you shouldn't pretend to. But you should treat everyone with respect. What matters above all is that you get out there and meet a lot of people.

Focus on the kind of people you need to meet—people who can hire you, for instance. You need a pretty big funnel to get enough clients to build a business. Remember that trucker I mentioned, whom I told to go out and meet people who needed trucking services? He didn't work for everyone he met. He didn't have to. He went out and met a lot of people who *might* need his services, developed relationships with a bunch of them, and then ended up working for several of the people he had really clicked with. Do you see the progression? You meet one hundred people, you develop relationships with fifty, you work with ten. The percentages will change depending on your niche, but it will always be a funnel.

And if you only know a dozen people, your funnel is too small.

Meeting people who can hire you is a good place to start when building a business or looking for work, but also when you're not yet looking or you're even just thinking about getting into a particular career. Start with the people who need your services, who are higher up than you are in your field. You need colleagues, of course, but a lot of people only focus on building relationships with colleagues instead of focusing on the people who actually pay or hire for the work you do.

You need to get out and actually meet—in person—people who might need you. Whatever your field is, focus on the decision makers, the business owners. Where do they hang out? Are they members of the Lions Club or the chamber of commerce? Can you go to their place of business just to introduce yourself and let them know that if they need someone in a pinch, you're available? Get yourself some business cards. Be polite and professional. Get out and meet them.

Of course you should also meet colleagues. If you're currently working in your field, you'll already know the people in your own department. Spread out; meet the people in other departments. Meeting people and developing a relationship with them before you need their help is a great way to ensure that they'll be there for you when you do need them. Participate in every get-together your office provides; the company picnic is a great way to relax, have fun, and make connections with people on your team but outside the narrow focus of what you do.

Meet people you can learn from. If there's someone who's already doing the kind of work you ultimately want to do, reach out to them. See if they'll give you a few minutes of their time to talk about how they started out. Always be willing to learn.

Finally, there's your community. You can be as deliberate and focused as you want in developing relationships, but nothing will ever beat the serendipity of working in the same soup kitchen as the vice president of the local savings and loan. Look to your church or your kid's school or any of the local volunteer groups and get out there and meet people. Building relationships in your community is good for your neighborhood and can also be good for your career.

Broadly going out and meeting people casts the widest possible net. You are looking for people who can help finance your projects, but you're also looking for reliable people you can hire when the time comes. Trust me when I tell you that finding a great manager is like finding gold. The bigger your list of contacts, the more likely you are to find the right person at the right moment, no matter what your goal may be.

## Be Open to Ideas

I've found that some people will only listen to their own ideas. If they didn't come up with it, they don't want to hear it.

What a waste.

The world is full of people with terrific ideas. Knowing a lot of people, and especially a lot of people in different walks of life, opens up vast resources of ideas if only you're willing to listen.

Listen to friends, to mentors, to your customers, to your staff. Reach out to individual stakeholders, people who have something on the line. Back when I worked for the credit union and needed to restructure the whopping 25 percent of the delinquent loans, I didn't just go in and make a blanket decision that we would restructure every loan one way. I certainly didn't want to foreclose on everyone. The decision I made was to talk personally with each individual whose loan was in trouble. I didn't lecture them, I listened to them. I made them see that we were in this together. I asked them what they needed to be able to meet their obligations. They were the experts on their situation. Our shared goal was for them to be able to meet their loans—and in the next section I'm going to talk about the importance of having a shared goal when you're negotiating. We were working together as partners to meet that goal; why wouldn't I listen to them? Why wouldn't I want them to show me how they could make this work? And by coming up with solutions together, they were more invested in a positive outcome than if I'd lectured them or created an antagonistic relationship. I wasn't an enemy, I was a partner. And as you'll recall, delinquent loans went down from 25 percent to 3 percent in three months.

## Negotiate So Everyone Wins

One of the biggest mistakes I see in the business world is when people negotiate, they think it's about "beating" the other person. They see it as a competition. So instead of creating a business relationship that is mutually beneficial, they create an adversarial relationship—and in doing so, they create an adversary. Why do they do this? Is it the thrill they get from "winning" a small battle? If so, it comes at the cost of winning what they really want.

Getting a reputation as being difficult, untrustworthy, or someone who takes advantage of others is not how you build wealth over the long term. I have had offers come back to me after they'd initially been rejected because the buyer they chose—who may have offered more money—proved to be impossible to deal with. I've had partners who have scuttled their own success by being arrogant and needing to be the "boss." A relationship will only thrive if both parties feel like their needs are being met. You need to approach any negotiation with that in mind. How do you negotiate a win-win?

First, of course, you have to know what you want—and how much you want it. This is critical. A negotiation requires a give-and-take on both sides. There are a lot of factors involved in any deal: time frame, cash up front, potential return on investment, even emotional factors. You need to figure out what really matters to you. What, for you, is a win?

Then you need to figure out what's a win for the other person. When buying properties, some people need cash fast, while other sellers want to take back a note on the property because it means steady, long-term income without the hassle of managing it themselves. Knowing what they really want gives you the ability to give it to them while getting them to bend on other things that are more important to you.

While money is always a motivation, it's not the only one. Some people want a bigger title or a better office, and will take those things instead of a raise. They want the things that signal success to others more than (or at least as much as) they want cash in hand. Or maybe they want to work from home or the freedom to take on other clients. People always want something underneath the obvious asking price or going rate. It's worth your time to investigate what that might be. Because if you can meet that, they'll be much more willing to meet your own needs.

My son, John, struggled at first with the concepts underpinning negotiations. There are a lot of moving parts: You have to go in with certain ideas, key points that matter to you, but you also have to go in with a certain flexibility. I'd prep him for a negotiation and I'm sure he thought I was nuts. Some of the things I said he should ask for or do or say must've seemed impossible. But he was open, he gave it a try, and it worked. John has told me that the creativity and boldness he learned negotiating helped him become the man he is today.

In addition to creating a win-win, another important factor in successful negotiations is your own personal integrity. It is absolutely essential that the people you're negotiating with believe that you will do what you say you'll do. Your integrity, your honesty, is the cornerstone of your ability to negotiate successfully. So how do you guarantee that they'll believe you?

Well, first of all, you don't lie.

You absolutely have to follow through on whatever it is you say you'll do. Your word must always be good. The minute you lie or cheat or misrepresent the truth, your integrity is gone. It's toast. Don't think word doesn't get around, because it does.

This is one of the things that makes no sense to me at all: people destroying their reputation for integrity. When other people know that you will do what you say you'll do, they're far more eager to work with you. For example, I had gotten a loan through a bank—a big loan, a million-dollar loan—and it was coming due. I didn't have the money; I needed another six months. What I did have going for me was the stellar relationship I had built with the bank manager. This relationship wasn't built on golfing and cocktails; it was built on trust. I had never lied or misrepresented a situation, no one had needed to foreclose on one of my loans, and I had in fact made them plenty of money over the years. He knew I was good for the money—I just wasn't good for it today. Convincing the manager to ignore bank policy and carry my million-dollar loan for another six months wasn't small potatoes, but it also wasn't that hard. I had carefully developed a reputation for honesty over years of working with people, and it was there to support me when I needed it.

It's a strength to be straightforward and honest, not a weakness. Develop this asset by negotiating deals where all parties get something they want, and always follow through on your word.

## Know Your Strengths

Once you have the foundations down, once you can read a contract and understand the numbers, that's when you get to look at your other strengths and see how you can best leverage them. So, what are your strengths?

# Expertise

Let's assume you are really great at something tangible. This could be anything, from design to accounting to writing press releases. There is some niche skill that you have down. How do you leverage that into a lucrative career?

The first step is to find out who will pay you for the work you do well. When I graduated from college as an accountant, I was able to walk right into a well-paying job with the IRS. This was important to me. My college mentor never got over the fact that I "sold out" and went to work for the government, but this was my life I was living, not hers. I had promised my first wife, Bernice, that if she supported us while I went to college full-time, I would support her once I graduated. We also wanted to start a family. My commitment to the life I wanted to have required a solid, steady job. And I also felt that this was a way to give back to my country. My parents were immigrants from Italy, and the United States had been very good to us. This was my chance to serve my country.

An unexpected bonus—one I lucked into, but you can actively seek out—was that by working for the IRS, I audited the books of a wide variety of businesses. If I'd gone to work for a private company— an advertising agency, a bank, an import/export company—I would quickly have become an expert in that one business, and that probably would have steered me down a particular path. Not that that's bad, but it wouldn't have worked for me. I like variety. Again, knowing yourself and your goals is key.

So who needs what you do well? Is there someone in an industry that excites you, someone farther along in their career, someone you can learn from? Or is there a type of business that could use your expertise across a variety of fields? Recognize that different opportunities exist with different choices.

If you're not an expert in a particular field, maybe what you offer is competence. A great assistant is an asset anywhere; instead of looking for the best salary, try looking for the experience that will give you the most opportunity. Even if what you want to do is move up a vertical ladder in one particular field, try to learn as much as you can about every department. And meet as many people as you can across the board.

# Connecting with People

Maybe navigating relationships isn't a skill you need to master. Maybe it's your greatest strength. You're what's called a "people person." You work well with others, you can get the best from everyone on your team, you know a lot of people in many different fields. If this is one of your top strengths, congratulations! You have a lot to leverage here.

The first thing you should do is decide that you will deliberately look for opportunities. This is a decision, a mindset. Whom do I want to work with? (Partners.) Who is doing what I want to be doing, and is there a way I can learn from them? (Mentors.) Whom can I help? (Protégées, and giving back to the community.) Make reaching out to others part of your daily routine.

The terrific thing about this skill is that it transcends industries. While I've made the bulk of my money in real estate, I have reached out to people my whole life, in every capacity. When I was just a kid dressing shop windows in Manhattan, I found a mentor who changed my life. How did I "find" him? I let him help me. He was someone with a lot of experience in a field that wasn't particularly prestigious or lucrative. Maybe he wasn't being interviewed by magazines and heralded as the next Rockefeller; so what? This was a guy who knew a lot of things that I didn't know. Why wouldn't I treat him with respect? He responded to that—and he noticed that when he gave me advice, I took it. I listened. I learned so much from him about the art of window dressing, but also about marketing, the importance of presentation, and how much aesthetics matter, all of which I've put into improving my real estate properties. When our department was cut, he sent me to North Carolina, where I blossomed. I want you to have someone in your life who does the same.

However, this is also an area where I see a lot of people fall down. I almost said "young people," but in fact, I've seen folks blow it at every stage of their careers. When someone gives you advice and you respond by being dismissive or defensive, you lose. Because they won't offer advice again. I don't care who you are, there is always something you can learn from someone else. But you have to be open to it. This is where making the decision to be on the lookout for mentors comes into play. If your default reaction to being given advice is to resist and pretend you already know it all, you will never "luck into" the mentorship that can change your life. You'll be too busy pushing it away.

I've also been open to helping out in my community, as well as finding individual people that I can mentor. I've trained my family in my business—everyone plays a part in the company now, right down the generations to my granddaughter, Natalie, who is my right hand in the office. But I've advised friends on properties they were considering, and of course I've been active on boards and for various charities and colleges. The key here is to give without expecting anything in return, but at the same time to be open to good things (and good people) if they show up. For instance, a contact I made while on the board at Pepperdine University became instrumental in helping me with a lifelong dream of educating people about the Italian culture. I publish those books through my foundation, The Mentoris Project. Did I join the board to scout out people I needed to make my projects happen? No. But did I recognize them when I met them? You bet I did. Again, it's about making a conscious choice to give back, and then also being on the lookout for opportunities and people you want to work with.

# Creativity

When I say to embrace creativity, I don't mean writing a symphony or painting watercolors—although if that's your thing, that's terrific. But creativity comes in many forms. Finding a way to make a deal work when the traditional way is blocked—that's very creative. I just did a deal to help someone flip a house and my kids were horrified. "Dad," they said, "there's no money in flipping houses in this market. What are you thinking?" But in fact, I structured the deal so that these guys, who are contractors, are doing all the improvements on the property for free. They're happy because they'll get their share when the house sells and I'm happy because I'll get my initial investment back plus interest plus a piece of the profit. It was a very creative deal in which they put no money down—so a big win for them—and I get a share of what will ultimately be a much more valuable property once they've made much-needed improvements.

Having a vision for how to improve something is extremely creative and a great skill. So is seeing different ways to make something happen despite obstacles, or ways to work together for everyone's benefit. And using creativity to add value to projects is always a plus. Your imagination allows you to see potential where right now there's just reality; your creativity allows you to realize that potential. Together, imagination and creativity direct your sails. It's up to you to put them to good use. Deliberately working to develop and use your creativity in business—and build a reputation as a creative thinker—is a terrific way to hone and leverage your skills.

## Hard Work and Focus

It could be that your greatest strength is that you are willing to work harder than everyone else. There are lots of ways to leverage that. First of all, if you excel in your day job, you will often be trusted to take on more challenging projects, ones where you can learn more and meet more decision makers. You are also capable of keeping side projects going even while working full-time, either at your own business or for someone else. Being willing to take on extra tasks, such as managing your apartment building, can keep money in your pocket—money you can invest in your next rental property.

Focus and hard work are important to your success. The trap is if you only work hard and focus on other people's businesses. You can be the world's greatest assistant, but if it keeps you stuck in someone else's hamster wheel, it's time to move on. Hard work needs to be in service of your greater goals. Put yourself in a position where you are constantly learning and growing as you work hard, and then be willing to move on when a better situation or the opportunity to work for yourself arises.

# Develop Multiple Sources of Income

For most people, that biweekly paycheck is the big moneymaker. It's the thing you count on to make rent and buy groceries. If you're following my suggestions, you are also socking part of it away to help you build your investment funds. In any event, earning that paycheck eats up a good forty hours per week, plus commute.

So what are you doing with the rest of your time?

Developing other sources of income will help you reach your goals more quickly. Of course the money is important; eventually, I want you to invest with OPM—Other People's Money—as much as possible, but that first investment is on you. You have to build a track record before people will trust you. So having a second or third income stream will help build your investment fund.

But having another source of income can provide other benefits. If you're working for yourself, you are running a business, whether it's lawn care in your neighborhood or selling handmade jewelry on Etsy. You have to learn how to keep your books, price your goods or services, do your taxes, maybe even hire extra help. A side business is a good place to learn the ropes and make your rookie mistakes.

If your day job isn't in the industry you want to work in—for instance, if you want to run your own restaurant, but you work in insurance—then a part-time job doing the books for a local restaurant can provide insight into that particular business. Again, be strategic. Bussing tables is also a restaurant job, and I'm not saying don't take it—just don't stay in it for long.

Working part-time in a new field also gives you the chance to meet people who are already established and playing at a higher level than you are right now. These are people who may become mentors, partners, or funders down the line. Do not blow the opportunity. Always be professional; excel at the job, no matter what it is. Shake hands, take names, and follow up.

A little bit here about being strategic: For the right opportunity, don't be afraid to start at the bottom. I've taken pay cuts to start in a new field in a less prestigious position and I've never regretted it. The key is you want to be someplace where you'll really learn the nuts and bolts of the business. And then you want to keep your eyes and ears open and actually learn. Skills translate; the visual marketing I learned by dressing windows in Manhattan directly impacts how I landscape my properties. But you have to be eager to learn.

So, to quickly recap, a second source of income can:

- Build your investment savings
- Teach you basic entrepreneurial skills
- Give you an insider's knowledge of a new industry
- Provide introductions to people who can help you down the line

What's the downside?

First of all, a lot of people don't like to work that hard. That was never me, and I hope it's not you. I'm not saying you can't succeed working just one job. I do think it will take longer. But, again, you have to live your life; you can't live mine. Let me suggest, however, that you want to align your life with your priorities.

If you are working in a lucrative job that is not what you ultimately want to do, then you definitely need to look for a way to work in your target industry as a consultant or even as a volunteer, at least for a little while. You may decide it's not right for you after all (such as when I was caddying at the golf course). Better to know that now rather than after you've quit your job to go all in on this new venture. And also—especially if you have a lucrative or comfortable job—you may never decide to leave; you can get trapped in a "good enough" life if you don't have a constant reminder of the life you really want. I spent my evenings and weekends taking care of my properties, and I was never happier. That happiness helped guide my decision-making, helped drive me to look for additional properties and ultimately to work solely for myself. Find what's fulfilling to you and make time to do it.

## Create Your Team

You need other people. For one thing, you won't be equally good at every aspect of the job. If you find someone better at a key component of your business than you are, for heaven's sake, hire them! For another, your time is valuable and finite. You simply can't do it all.

Just like with partners, you need to make sure that everyone shares your values and vision. When I'm looking to hire anyone, even a gardening service for one of my buildings, I want someone who works hard and sees the same potential for the complex that I see. Why would I hire someone who didn't want to plant flowers when flowers are something I care about having at all of my buildings? I wouldn't. Just as I wouldn't want to hire someone who didn't have the core value of taking pride in their work. It really matters to hire people who align with your mission in life.

You will make mistakes. You will work with people who don't understand what you're looking for or why you are investing, and so they'll show you the wrong apartments or mess up the contract or not bother to check the roof. This is part of why you need to educate yourself in all aspects of your business, so that you can see when someone is doing you a disservice. They may not be bad at their job, they're just a bad fit for you. Don't buy the building; don't sign the contract. You don't have to lay blame, just chalk it up to a learning experience, shake their hand, and walk away. You don't want to burn bridges, but you certainly don't want to waste any more of your time.

The opposite is also true: When you find someone who understands what you're going for and is willing to work with you, keep them. Develop the relationship so that both of you can succeed together on bigger and better projects. This is especially important with institutions like banks. You are never really going to a bank for a loan—you are always going to a specific person at that bank. See it as a relationship that will continue to be beneficial to both of you and nurture it. Your loan officer is as much a part of your team as your manager or your plumber.

I wish there were a way to tell you how you can recognize great people and only work with them, but I can't. There's no secret handshake that people with good values and expertise have to introduce themselves. I can tell you, though, that this is one of the reasons you invest in relationships. This is one of those things I mentioned, something that lives in nuances. You can learn how to recognize kindred spirits by connecting with other people, as well as by learning from your mistakes.

The other thing you can do—something I have learned always to do—is verify. Start with a small project or the first step of a project and then make sure they do what they say they'll do. If so, move onto the next step. If not, well, you've kept the damage to a minimum.

Trust, but verify.

Building your team also means being strategic about those you meet. You shouldn't just begin looking for gardeners, say, after escrow has gone through. Evaluate the landscaping on every property you visit. Is it the kind of thing you want? Is it kept up the way you want it? Ask people who their landscapers are and whether or not they like working with them. Open-ended questions are great; people love to talk, but if you just ask them how much someone costs, that's all they'll give you. You want to ask broader questions, things like how they found the company and do they like the workers, has it been a good experience, how much they have to oversee them, that kind of thing. Get them talking and really listen to their answers. You can build a list of potential team members for every job before you need them so you're not scrambling when you do.

## CASE STUDY

## The Restaurant

I've mentioned a couple of times that I was a partner in a restaurant/bar—technically, a partner in the land it sat on, since that was the deal I had helped to create. I could have walked away as soon as the deal was signed and let them run the restaurant because my job was done. I had no direct stake in the restaurant's success. But there very quickly arose a real problem: The manager we'd hired to run the place turned out to be unreliable in the extreme; two months after the restaurant opened, we had to fire him. We needed someone competent, level-headed, and business-savvy.

We needed me.

At the time, although I was busy with my own properties and investments, I didn't have a day job. I like to be busy and I love a new challenge, and I would be managing the restaurant for a paycheck. This meant that the money from our investments could be funneled into the purchase of another property, and you know my feelings about that. So, on paper, this looked like a great idea.

I took on the job with gusto. I kept the books, ordered the food, managed the staff, and of course instantly started to implement changes to improve the quality of the restaurant and—not coincidentally—its return on investment.

This is a great example of listening to individual stakeholders. I started by talking to the people who worked in the restaurant every day. The waitresses hated their dingy uniforms. Sharp uniforms meant better tips. I told them they could have whatever uniform they wanted to wear if they would pay for it themselves; I would take a little bit out of their paychecks every week until it was paid off. They instantly saw the value in this: They could wear a sharp, new uniform with pants instead of a skirt; they would be more comfortable; plus they would look more professional and their tips would increase, easily covering their out-of-pocket costs for the uniforms. The waitresses were happy, the customers were happy, and the restaurant instantly took on a more professional look, so I was happy. You know who wasn't happy?

My partners.

These guys didn't bother to talk to the waitresses. They wanted them wiggling around the place in short skirts and strenuously objected to them wearing pants. They weren't willing to listen to anyone else; if it wasn't their idea, they didn't like it. Luckily, in this case, they didn't get a vote. The new uniforms stayed.

Don't be those guys. Don't shut yourself off to other people's insights. There were solid reasons why the new uniforms were a great idea, reasons I wouldn't have thought of myself. Reaching out to the waitresses, to the people immediately involved in the decision, gave me valuable information and improved our team and our product. Don't let your ego cut you off from good ideas.

The most important source of information comes from people directly affected by a situation. A local newspaper columnist suggested we give a free appetizer to customers while they waited for their order. This person was a customer; he hit upon a solution to a problem we were facing, but also a way to differentiate ourselves from all the other restaurants in town. I mean, who gives out free food? But let me tell you, the cost of the appetizer was won back a hundred times over. We contacted the local paper to tell them about this new promotion, they covered it, and our bookings increased by 50 percent. Can you imagine? It was a stunning success to get that many extra dinners and drinks and desserts for the cost of a plate of appetizers per table. Brilliant. And it came from someone who experienced too long a wait for their food.

Running the restaurant was all-encompassing. I left the house at six in the morning and made it home about nine at night. It was grueling, but especially in that first year, I really made a difference.

The problem was that my hours never got better. I continued to work all the time. This is the one time in my life when I forgot that wealth was not about money, or even about making a success of the restaurant. This truth was brought home to me one day when, of all people, Bernice walked into the restaurant. She had our three children with her. She lined them up in front of me and said, "Take a good look. That's your father."

Point taken.

I had been earning good money for a family I essentially hadn't seen in two years. That was not the life I wanted to live. That was not wealth; it's never money over family. I knew right then it was time to move on, and I did.

This is the story I wanted to share with you not just because it shows how you can be creative and successful by listening to your team and being willing to try new ideas, but also because I believe the greatest mistake you can make is that in the excitement of building something new, you can sometimes lose sight of your true values. My family was the most important thing to me, and while it was my job to provide for them financially, it was also my job to be there for them, in person, more than once in a blue moon.

## Making Mistakes

I've made a lot of mistakes over the years. I've moved too quickly on a project, I've trusted people I shouldn't, I've fallen in love with properties that weren't a good fit for my business. Most of these I've chalked up to a learning experience. We all make mistakes; if we learn from them and do better the next time, they were worth the trouble. This, by the way, is why I recommend working with someone on a small project or limiting the risks of your first big investment. Make your mistakes before there's too much on the line. Here are some to watch out for:

- Get it in writing. If someone offers to make you a partner down the line, do not lift a finger until you have a signed deal. Because the more successful you are, the less they'll want to share a piece of something profitable. For any situation, no matter what the verbal understanding is, it's not real until the contract is signed.

- Make sure you understand the fine print. This wasn't my mistake, but one I saw my mother make. She understood the numbers, but English was not her first language. The men she worked with put in clauses that gave them rights she would never have agreed to had she fully understood them, and they enforced them. My mother recovered and was still making twice as much money as I was after I graduated from college; again, learning from your mistakes makes you stronger. But trust me when I say it's critical to understand every line before you sign your name.

- Don't assume someone else is doing their job. Again, my mother got into legal trouble because her lawyer didn't file some papers in time. Work with the best possible people, trust their judgment, but keep tabs on them, especially if a deadline is looming. I've said it before, but it's a great mantra for working with others: Trust, but verify.

- Be careful of bad habits. As a teenager, I had friends who gambled their paychecks every week. They'd gamble on boxing matches, on cards, on anything they could bet on. I realized very quickly that this was the way to ruin. Drinking to excess will destroy your life—and if you're behind the wheel of a car, it can destroy the lives of others as well. My brother died of lung cancer. These choices—to pick up a drink or a cigarette or to put down a bet—aren't building your wealth. They are destroying your health and your chance to succeed in life. I'm not immune to bad habits. Overwork has caused me a lot of stress and health issues over the years. It wasn't until I started working for myself that the stress vanished. Making my own decisions was the best decision I ever made, but even so, I have to be careful to take the occasional break.

- Live beneath your means. It's not just about saving money to invest, it's about living without the stress of being overextended. Stress over money can ruin your health, gut your marriage, and destroy your family. Living above your means is gambling that nothing bad will ever happen, because if it does, you won't have the resources to meet it. Let me tell you, that is a bet you will never win.

You will make mistakes. I hope you won't make the ones I've listed above, but you might. You'll probably make new ones, too. That's okay. Learn from them. You also need to get over making a mistake as quickly as you can. For me, what helps is assigning a dollar value to it. I ask myself, okay, how much is this going to cost me? How much will it cost to walk away, refinance, or regroup? I factor in my time and any real costs, and I give it a number. Then I factor that into my financial plan for the next six months to a year, and I move on.

It's just a number. Learn what you can, put it behind you, and focus on the next thing.

# RECAP: MASTERY

- **Create your own path to success.** Map foundational skills onto your particular situation and see what you still need to learn. At a bare minimum, you will need to be able to read a contract, understand the numbers, develop relationships, negotiate so that everyone wins, and leverage your strengths.

- **Develop multiple sources of income.** Ideally, your various projects will provide income and opportunities to learn about your industry, meet the right people, and develop your entrepreneurial skills.

- **Build a team of people who can help you get what you want.** Even if they're "on the bench" for now, you should be meeting and evaluating people who can fund your projects, manage your business, build your website, landscape your properties, organize your files—and on and on, a thousand things that will need to be done, depending on what industry you go into. Always be on the lookout for smart, competent, creative people who share your values and work with them whenever you can.

- **Try something new.** Make mistakes. Learn from them. Keeping track of what works and what doesn't leads to mastery.

# Chapter Six

## Family Development

Family has always come first for me. The times I chose work over family (and to be fair, I was working to provide for my family—it never started out as an either/or proposition), I recognized my mistake and I changed course. What is ultimately the point of wealth if not to be able to spend time with the people you love?

So if real wealth is about having a life full of family, friends, and independence, how can you accomplish that? Can you build a family the way you build a business?

Well, yes and no.

## Partners

I've already told you how Bernice was the first woman I ever met who shared my vision for my life. I never had any doubt that she was the one I wanted to marry, and we were happy together every day. I want that for you, too. To me, that's real wealth.

The problem is that most people don't even have a shared vision for their life as one of the top three requirements for choosing a spouse. You're supposed to look for a gal who's pretty or a guy who's a good provider or someone who's nice. What does any of that matter? You could be a great person and you could marry a great person and the two of you can still be miserable together because fundamentally you want to lead different lives. Where's the wealth in that?

Marriage is, at heart, a lifelong partnership. If you're not partnering for a common goal, you're going to have a rough time of it. Knowing what you want before you get involved with someone is important, because otherwise how can you know if they want what you want? And then, of course, you need to make sure that your potential partner does know what they want, and isn't just saying what they think you want to hear.

Nuances. Learning to read people. It comes in handy in your personal life as well as in business.

Your marriage is going to be the single most important partnership of your life. Too many people go into it without talking about the big questions. "Do you want kids?" is one. But "What does wealth mean to you?" is another. "What's your vision of success?" "What is enough?" This is the time to work out the nitty-gritty details of your lives together, to make sure you have the same expectations, from how you'll share household duties to what your political and religious beliefs are. Don't expect the other person will change who they are to suit you once you're married.

Bernice and I talked a lot when we were courting, and we kept talking through our entire marriage. She was involved in all of our financial decisions. Usually, she was telling me I didn't have enough money to buy a particular property, and I was proving her wrong. That was part of the fun. She was the realist and I was the creative deal-maker. Together, we made a great team, and after she passed away, I lost my zest for life for a long time.

I was very lucky to find a second life partner who is also kind-hearted and supportive and shares my vision. It was my privilege to marry Josephine in 2003, and she has made the last sixteen years very happy ones. Together, our partnership centers on family and philanthropy, on helping others, and in many ways this book is an outgrowth of that. She's been very involved, reading each draft and supporting me in my belief that through this medium, we can help other people find real wealth.

The thing about partnerships—in marriage as in business—is first, as I've said, you have to pick the right partner. But second, you must nurture that partnership. Be a great partner yourself. Be honest, be open, make sure you're communicating. Does this sound like marriage counseling? Not to brag, but I've had two very good marriages—maybe there's something here you should listen to! But all kidding aside, think of how you would want a business partner to treat you: with respect, with transparency, letting you in on the small problems they're encountering rather than waiting until things are in crisis mode. That's the kind of business partner you want, and certainly the kind you should be. Why would you treat your life partner with any less than that level of respect and honesty?

## Negotiations

They say everything in life is a negotiation. I don't know if that's true, but it's certainly true within a family. And in no other situation is it more important that, at the end of the negotiation, everyone feels like a winner.

Because you're going to have to work with these folks for the rest of your life.

Too many people make work/family a dichotomy. I don't believe in that at all. It's not either/or; it's not a zero-sum game between work and family. I think your work + your family = your life, and if you want a life filled with wealth, you'd better make sure that both sides of the equation are happy.

You do that by making sure everyone feels they are a valued member of the team. You and your partner are still in charge, of course; this is not a democracy where majority rule means ice cream for breakfast. But people need to feel heard. Your kids need to have agency. Everyone needs to be enrolled in the family's vision, the family's goals. My son, John, says that working with his mom and me in the business from a very young age brought him a lot of pride and hope for the future. By second grade, he was already looking to business as a career, and let me tell you, he already had experience in the trenches, even then.

Communication is the key to learning. How can you expect your children to learn your values or foundational skills if you don't communicate them? I don't just mean talking to them, although of course you're doing that. Skills and values are learned even faster when your children are active participants; they learn by doing.

This is true with negotiations. When you are negotiating properly, you're learning what matters to the other person and you are communicating what your own position is. You're treating the other party with respect and honesty, and you are making it clear that they should do the same with you. Why wouldn't you want to teach your teenager those skills?

Negotiation can also be a pathway to a strong relationship. When you negotiate with someone, whether it's a buyer or a vendor or a twelve-year-old, you are building a bridge not just to each other, but to a shared future. Let's say you're buying a house. You and the seller are both working toward the shared goal of the house being sold. They have other goals: They want the most money they can get for it, and maybe they want to sell quickly because they have to move out of state for work, or maybe they need to rent back from you for a few months until their kid has graduated high school. When you understand their position, it makes you more able to meet their needs and have your needs met in return. It's never a simple adversarial goal based on the sale price—or if it is, you were probably too lazy or too focused on your own goals to create a win for the other person. The outcome is that you will both lose.

The same is true with your spouse and your kids. Negotiating wins so that everyone is clear on the shared goal, enrolled in making it happen, and feels that their own needs are met creates a family team that can depend upon each other. And here, as in business, your power to negotiate is in direct proportion to your integrity. If people don't believe you'll be true to your word, they're less willing to give ground on the things that matter to you.

Don't lie to your business partners or your life partners or your kids. Move together toward that shared goal.

# The Family Budget

One of the greatest gifts you can give your children is a strong financial education. Someday those kids will be adults and have families of their own to support; if they have no idea how to read a profit/loss statement or invest their savings or budget their resources, they will not thrive.

Teach them to fish while they're young and they'll never go hungry. The same is true for budgeting. My daughter Patty and her husband bought a triplex before they bought their first home. She tells me that one of the things she learned from us was that you always need to have a back-up plan financially. At the end of every year, her family sits down to review their financial goals for that year, develop their goals for the next, and set their budget. They have both a five- and a ten-year plan in place. And they meet those goals.

It's also important for your kids to learn that money doesn't buy happiness. I know people say that so often that it's in one ear and out the other. That's why you can't just tell them—you have to show them. Take them to the park, go on family hikes, play catch. None of these things will break the bank, but all of them will lead to memories they'll cherish forever. And then talk about it. Talk about how you didn't need money to have fun. Make the connection for them between time together and joy. Money isn't a factor in that equation.

You should also sit down and share the family budget. Because by now you've done one, right? If not, do it now. This is a learning opportunity not just for you, but for the next generation, for the kids you'll someday unleash on the world. Do us all a favor and teach them how to budget.

Your budget isn't just about saving money to invest later. You also need emergency savings. You need to save money for college for each of your kids. And you don't have to live like hermits. Don't say, "Barbera told me all my money had to go to savings, so it's ramen noodles for dinner again, kids." Don't be ridiculous. Consider realistic spending patterns. Create limits on lifestyle expenses, but recognize that everyone's needs should be met.

The other thing is that doing a budget in conjunction with your family will put into play all of those negotiation skills we were talking about. Negotiation is about both parties having a shared outcome that they want. My kids might not have been invested in their parents buying a particular property, but they were always invested in the family success that we were all working toward.

Remember I mentioned that Bernice's first thought when we hit a million in revenue was that she was worried our money would spoil the kids? Bernice was a great mother, and of course her first thoughts were for our children.

But I wasn't too worried. The kids hadn't grown up with all the trappings of wealth; our savings were too important to us when they were young to spend on keeping up with the Joneses. They understood that we were investing in our shared future together. If later, they got some things that they hadn't had when they were growing up, it was in the context of "Work hard now, reap rewards later." I think that solidified the message rather than undercutting it.

And if how our kids turned out is any indication, I think Bernice was worried for nothing. My daughter Ann says one of the things she learned from me was that I always seem to allow money to flow through me—I've never hoarded it for myself and I've always looked for ways to share it with family and charities. I was really touched by this. That's not a spoiled kid talking. That's a person I am proud to have given to the world.

## A Family Business

I brought each of my kids into the property management business as early as I could. Here's what we did: As a family—for fun—we would go to visit properties for sale. Some families go to yard sales on Saturday mornings. We went to property sales.

But the kids weren't just dragged around or left outside to play. From the beginning, Bernice and I showed them what we were looking for and especially what the warning signs were. Each child ended up developing an expertise in a particular area. As soon as they'd grasped the essentials, we sent them off to evaluate and report back on, say, the plumbing. Of course we went over their report with them, checking to see if it was accurate or what they might have missed. We did that dozens of times. But then we didn't anymore. Once we knew that they knew what they were doing, that they were exhaustive and accurate, we trusted them, and we let them know it.

We made them part of the team.

It's not that Bernice and I didn't make mistakes as parents—I've already told you about my whopper, spending two years running a restaurant instead of being with my family—but we did a couple of things right. First, Bernice and I were always a united front. We rarely disagreed anyway, and never on anything important, but we really were one voice with the kids. We never undercut each other.

Bernice was also a terrific role model. Patty vividly remembers her mother's drive and persistence. How whenever she got knocked down in life, she got right back up. How she took care of our children *and* took care of the bookkeeping. For Bernice, running the business was part of raising her family. There were setbacks, but never failures.

Another thing we did right was that we provided the opportunity for our kids to be part of the team. We gave them opportunities, early and often, to take pride in their work and to see that we took pride in them for that. My son, John, has a terrific ability to notice things the rest of us miss, particularly when it comes to potential problems with a property. He can see beyond the obvious, and that's a skill I've been grateful to have on our team. On his side, John told me that he's learned many things from me, and he appreciates the lessons, the hard work, and the love. This is one of the great joys of bringing your children into the family business.

Bernice and I gave our children the ability to grow within our business rather than grow resentful of a business that took us away from them. Eventually, the kids were surveying the rent on potential properties, checking out deferred maintenance issues, and developing loan applications. They also were treating tenants and employees with the same respect we did. This is another thing you pass on: not just knowledge, not just the importance of being diligent, but the respect for other people that you yourself show.

And we benefited from our children's growing expertise. Obviously, there was the benefit of being able to send a team of trusted advisers into the building so we didn't have to look at every little detail ourselves. We could clear a building in record time and know almost immediately if it was a potential investment or not. Having expert minions saves a lot of time! But we also benefited as human beings, Bernice and I, as parents. We got to spend time with our children. By providing them with a structure for taking responsibility and developing a work ethic, we were able to help them grow up to be strong, capable human beings. What a pleasure that was, as a parent, to watch that happen.

That's real wealth right there.

## Valuing Others

When I talk about the "family business," there are actually two branches of family: my blood relatives and my employees. It is incredibly important not just to hire people you like and respect, but also to make sure they feel like they're part of your family. We recognize our employees for their years of service every five years, and we hold a picnic and a Christmas party annually. We appreciate them. This makes good business sense by keeping turnover low and reducing the frequency of training new people, but that's not why we do it. We do it because it matters to have a bond with the people who actually make your company work.

You know that I'm all about fulfilling the vision you have for your life. I really don't think anything else is worth doing. But fulfilling your vision is worthless if you step all over the people around you in doing so. Be respectful of everyone's time and efforts, from your most junior assistant to the bank manager to the contractor fixing your roof. Create good vibes; appreciating people will make them flourish around you. This, too, makes good business sense (that junior assistant may be running the company in a few years), but it's also the right thing to do, the ethical way to be. You have to live with people, and the person you have to live with forever is yourself. Trust me when I tell you that ethical people are much easier to live with!

Also, things are going to go wrong. From the stories I've already told, you know that I've made mistakes, trusted the wrong people, or given my all to something that ultimately gave me little in return. Those things happen; they're the cost of being out in the world. They only become a problem when you can't let go.

The time and energy people waste regretting situations that are over and done with is ridiculous. Why are you still complaining about something that happened months ago? You can walk away from something, but that doesn't always mean you can leave it behind you. I'm not a psychologist, so I'm not going to get into why people do this. I'll only tell you that this is a waste, a terrible waste, of your limited time on earth.

I may not forget—hey, I'm not a saint—and even if I can't quite forgive, I can always move on. I always look to what I've learned from a situation or a person, even if it ended badly. I can do this because I can separate out the good from the other things that happened. And this is key: I can value the good. Even when a partnership or a project or a situation has left a bad taste in my mouth, I can value the good that was there or the things that I learned. This makes it much easier to let it go.

Value others. Appreciate what you've learned in a situation. You do this not for them, but for you. You need all your energy focused on your next accomplishment, on the next deal, the next business, the next iteration of your career. You simply can't afford to dwell on the negative.

Nowhere is this more important than with your own family.

It's easy to take the people you see every day for granted. It's easy to get caught up in the cycle of resentment or exhaustion when you're working a day job, running a side business, and coaching your kid's T-ball team. Taking the time to deliberately value these people who share your life with you—that's priceless. It's an investment of time and energy that will return to you tenfold in joy and peace.

## Valuing Yourself

Valuing yourself is just as important as appreciating those around you. Your confidence, your sense of self-worth, those things come from knowing you are doing good in the world and not just doing well. They come from recognizing that you have something to contribute.

Value yourself. Be like my father—charge well for your expertise, do a brilliant job, and make sure they understand that what you do is unique. Don't give yourself away to anyone who wants a piece of you. Put a premium on your time and make sure it's being spent in a way that supports your own true wealth. Give time to family, to children, to community, and to building your business. Value yourself enough to say no to anything that doesn't support your vision for your life.

There is another way to value yourself: life insurance. I absolutely believe that insurance is a measure of your commitment to your family and your love for them. Terrible things that are out of your control can and do happen. Would you really want your family to lose their home, their business, and their future in addition to losing you?

Of course not. Buy life insurance. Don't let people talk you out of it. I had friends who told me what a waste of money it was, how there were far better ways of using those funds. The thing was that they didn't follow through themselves and use that premium money for "better" investments. Meanwhile, when inflation hit, I was paying my premiums with cheaper dollars. But you know what? In the end, that's not what mattered. I wasn't buying life insurance because it was a good investment; I was buying it because I loved my family enough to protect them.

I bought mortgage insurance for the same reason. Given that for a long time we carried mortgages on investment property while I was also the breadwinner, I needed to make sure that if something happened to me, there would be no mortgage debt. I'm a risk-taker, but I can take risks in my business because I take none with the safety and security of my family. It's what I was talking about back in the section on assessing your risk tolerance: A lot of things we think of as risky can be mitigated. And that gives us the freedom to do what we need to do.

## True Wealth

To me, money is just a tool. It's something I use to build the life I want.

Money is also replaceable. My parents went bankrupt not once, but twice. I have been in some tight spots financially, walked away from good-paying jobs, and made financial mistakes aplenty. None of those things are permanent. If you have the foundations for success, money will keep coming back to you.

That's not true about people.

People are unique, and the people you love are irreplaceable. This is something you may know intellectually, but you really feel it viscerally when someone you love dies. When my mother passed, and my father, and Henry—those were blows that I'll never fully recover from. And when Bernice passed away in 2001, I thought my world had come to an end. We'd been married for forty-five years; she was my rock.

This was the one time I really lost any desire to move forward on a business level. I couldn't even go home for a week after Bernice's memorial service; I stayed with my daughters. This is when it hit home to me that wealth had very little to do with money. It took a long while for me to get out of this enveloping sadness. One of the things that helped was focusing on charities and ways I could contribute to others. My children were also there for me. And then, I was lucky enough to find love a second time with my wonderful Josephine. But there's no question that when Bernice passed, I had to come to terms with the fact that in life, there is always an end.

Cherish the people you love while you have them. Give them your time and attention, and incorporate them into every part of your life. When they're gone, remember and appreciate the times you had and the good things they brought to your life. Wealth isn't static, not monetarily and not in terms of happiness, health, or love.

## RECAP: FAMILY DEVELOPMENT

- **Your spouse is your partner in work and in life.**
  Make sure they share your vision for the future before you tie the knot.

- **Negotiations are always about looking for the shared goal and making sure everyone wins.** Nowhere is this more important than in your own family.

- **Budgeting = financial freedom.** Educate your children on the power of a budget.

- **Your spouse is your partner and your family is your team.** Rather than splitting work and family into two competing parts of your life, see how you can enlist their support. Build your family into the family business.

- **Value yourself and appreciate the contributions of others to your life.**

- **True wealth is sharing your success with the people you love.**

# CHAPTER SEVEN

## POWER EARNING

You work hard for your money, but real wealth comes when your money works hard for you.

Today, everyone's looking for passive income, a way to scale their business, a way to make money that's not simply exchanging time for dollars. There's a good reason for this: There are only so many billable hours in a day. Your income, if you rely exclusively on billing for your own efforts, is bound by time and destined to end. Could you financially weather a major health crisis? If something took you off of work for six months or a year, what would your family do?

You already know I think of wealth as independence. But if you are dependent on a single paycheck, however large—or one breadwinner, whatever the salary—you and your family are not independent. You don't have true wealth if you don't even have the freedom to get sick or take a real vacation, or retire. You have skills, you have knowledge, you have (I hope) a cushion of savings to invest. What's next for you is deciding how best to put your money to work for you.

## Leveraging Your Skills

By now, you are an expert in something. Maybe it's drawing up contracts or building websites or raising money or doing anything else people need. There's something out there that you are more than good at. What is it? Identifying your expertise is the first step to being able to leverage it.

"Wait a minute, Robert," I can hear you say. "I thought this was about leveraging my money." Sure, and we'll get to that. But let's start with rethinking what your own value is before we jump into cold, hard cash.

Remember in the very first chapter, when I talked about the mindset of wealth? This is a mindset shift you need to make. You need to think about how you can leverage what you already do not just to make more money (get a raise, get a promotion, start a side job), but to make money in a different way. I want you to start looking for potentially lucrative projects in which your investment is in skill, not cash.

For instance, start looking for places you can trade your skill for partnership or equity. I became a one-third partner in the restaurant because I was able to put the land deal together for my colleague and his silent partner. My connections and real estate expertise were what they needed to make their vision happen. In exchange, I became a one-third partner in the land deal without investing any capital. Look for ways you can leverage your expertise for a piece of the action, as they say, rather than being paid upfront.

A few things to keep in mind. First, be smart about your compensation. For instance, they initially offered me a piece of the restaurant, but I knew the real money was in the land. I let them share the restaurant fifty-fifty, which made them happy, but I was well rewarded for the work I did for them when it came time to buy me out of my third of the land, the value of which had appreciated greatly over the years.

Second, you will make some mistakes. You will give your time and expertise to projects that never find funding or have principals who don't have the stamina or smarts to make it over the initial challenges. That's okay. You may invest time and expertise without being fairly compensated, but you've also probably made some new connections at a high level. You have learned whom you can trust and who is just trying to look like a player. If you have done a great job and have been professional throughout, you can come out of it with relationships intact and some new knowledge under your belt.

To that end, try to pick projects that have some upside even if the business itself collapses. For instance, if you're considering bringing someone into one of your own companies or a new partnership, doing something small with them first will offer you the opportunity to see them under pressure. Remember my motto *Trust, but verify*? Helping someone out with your expertise is a low-risk way to verify that they are all you thought they were, and to uncover any potential pitfalls in the relationship before you've made a big investment.

Finally, get your understanding in writing. Never rely on a verbal agreement. Get in writing what your compensation will be, especially if it's deferred, and what your position within the new company or project will be, including your title, your share of the profits, your ownership in terms of decision-making and final say. You may not have any decision-making ability, and that's okay, so long as you know it in advance. The point of a contract is to bring expectations out into the open before the work is done or the investment is made. Problems arise in every situation, in every field, when both partners have different expectations that they haven't articulated.

Don't sell yourself short, either. You may not be investing cash, but you are investing time and expertise. That has value and should be compensated. Go ahead and take some fliers on people and projects that interest you, but be sure that when they make money, you will, too.

## Leverage Your Offer

What do you have to offer that's unique? What does your company offer that no one else can match? Once you know what that is, you can leverage that to land more clients and grow your business.

When I was with the credit union, they were stagnating, yet they offered a huge dividend of 6 percent, far more than depositors could get anywhere else. That was one of my key selling points, and I made hay with it. Everything else was gravy. When I was leasing cars, my focus was on making it an easy yes. We combined a low price point with a simple contract; other companies had long contracts and dickering, but with us, everything was geared toward simplicity. And when I first struck out on my own as a tax consultant, the selling point was clear: I had worked for the IRS and knew how to maximize your tax benefits while keeping you scrupulously on the right side of the law. Pinpointing what you offer and using that as a selling point doesn't just bring clients, it brings you the kind of clients you want to have. Tax scofflaws need not apply.

# CASE STUDY

## Starting a Leasing Business from Scratch

This is a good time to give you the full details of my foray into the car leasing business. Not because it was a wild success, although in many ways it was, but because of the experience it brought me. I gave you a quick overview earlier, but this is where I want you to learn from both what I did right and what I did wrong.

First, here's what I did right.

I was always on the lookout for new opportunities. I also always threw myself into whatever job I had. So even as I was buying apartment buildings and enrolling my family in managing them, I was also working a day job at a car dealership with my usual level of passion. I did what I always do: make friends, excel at the accounting, and look for ways to improve the workflow.

None of this went unnoticed. My boss reached out to me with a proposition: What if the two of us went into partnership together on a new business? Instead of selling cars outright, what if we leased them as well?

This was a perfect situation for me. It was the

opportunity to run a new business, do things my way, set it up to be efficient and effective right from the start. I would be paid a salary for managing the office, and I would also be given a partnership once it was up and running. For me, this was a no-brainer. Of course I said yes.

I've already talked about how I scoped out the competition and simplified contracts, which was a win both for our customers and for our team. But I learned something else from going to all of those other leasing companies: I learned which customers were being well served and which were being left behind.

Of course I focused on those left behind.

At the time, the high-end leasing business was booming. There were many companies out there leasing premium cars to people who could afford them. The people with fewer options were of lower- and middle-class incomes, who either couldn't afford or didn't want to lease a high-end car. Those were the people I built our company to serve.

First I went to Bank of America, and on the strength of the dealership's success was able to secure a line of credit to branch out into leasing. Then I looked at the various car manufacturers. I wanted to work with someone who needed me, a company with something to gain by helping me.

I found Toyota.

Toyota was very new to the United States market at that time. They were hot to have cars brought in, and so they were extremely reasonable. I worked with them to acquire the cars at a very low price. The line of credit was available, so I could move forward quickly. I had low overhead because I wasn't paying for the lot;

it was an unused space owned by the dealer. I hired a salesman who worked on commission only. The one place we spent good money was in advertising. My friend who owned the dealership gave me great advice on how to advertise. People poured into the lot trying to figure out how we could possibly be leasing a car at the advertised price.

The low price point was key. We didn't want to be in direct competition with the leasing companies in Beverly Hills—although more than one tried to hire me away! But we were never going to make money with big markups because that wasn't the type of client we served. I was looking for people who wanted something economical. We were able to offer inexpensive leases on solid cars and make up in volume what we didn't make in profit on a single vehicle. Some leasing companies were happy if they leased two cars a week; we leased two to three cars every day. Less profit per car, but exponentially more cars.

Most leasing companies also had a policy of telling you how much you owe on the lease only when you bring the car back; it depended on how much the car had kept its value while you were driving it. Needless to say, this was a pain point for customers—you didn't know until you turned it in how much more you were going to have to shell out. But I realized that Toyotas were great cars that really held their value, so instead of haggling at the end of the lease, I guaranteed up front how much you would have to pay when the lease was over. There were no unpleasant surprises for the client, and I set up a solid business in wholesaling the pre-leased Toyotas. The key to our success at every stage was volume, and the key to that was creating an obvious win for someone who leased from us rather than our competitors.

Toyota, by the way, was thrilled with our success because they wanted to break into the U.S. market. Every driver who leased one of our cars was a potential sale down the line. They didn't make much money selling to us, but again, the volume was high. Also, they made a great car and they had faith that many of our drivers would end up purchasing a Toyota later. They were building customer loyalty while we were building our company.

People came into our leasing company because they saw the incredible price we offered on leasing a Toyota, but not everyone wanted that car. Our ads and our price-leader got them in the door, but some of them wanted to drive an American-made car, or a car a notch above the economy Toyota. I had deals with both a Chevy and a Cadillac dealer that if someone came in and wanted to upgrade to a better car, they would sell me the car wholesale to lease. The dealers would even find the car my client wanted in the system because I was guaranteeing them a sale. You had to be careful that you weren't doing anything that could be construed as a bait-and-switch, which is unethical and illegal. In other words, you can't bring people in with the promise of a Toyota economy car and then start upselling them a Cadillac. But if they come in, look at the Toyota, and say, "You know, I really want a Chevy," then you can ethically provide them with what they want.

To say that starting a leasing company was a learning experience would be an understatement. I built a successful company from scratch and I did it by leveraging my dealership experience, my creativity, and my work ethic. In the process, I learned not only about the car leasing business, but how to implement all the strategies I'd learned from auditing other people's businesses. This was my chance to try, hands-on, all the best practices I'd gleaned over the years. Take a second to look at all the skills you need to have in place: negotiation, research, relationships, leveraging other people's money (in this case, a line of credit from the bank), creating wins for your partners and your clients . . . . Launching a business requires firing on all cylinders.

And it worked. Almost immediately, I was able to build a profitable business that was a win for the customer and a win for our company, and furthermore rewarded customers for being good people, taking care of the cars, and acting with integrity. It was everything I'd hoped for both in terms of success and in terms of validation that, yes, I could run my own company.

Now here's what I did wrong.

My old boss funded the project. My sweat equity, his capital—it was supposed to be an equal partnership. But I didn't get that in writing. He would promise, I would believe him, and then nothing would materialize. The more successful I was, the less he wanted to share that success with me.

Having said that, I did a couple of other things right. First, I left. When it became clear that he was not going to honor his commitment to make me a full partner, I just turned in my keys and walked away. I did not stay on, hoping he would change his mind or trying to do an even better job to prove my worth. I knew my worth. And if I wasn't going to be recognized for it,

I certainly wasn't going to be able to continue working there. I give my all in everything I do, but I can't give my all in that kind of situation.

If you find yourself resenting your boss or in a position where you're not ever going to be fully compensated—or, I would even say, if you find yourself with someone who doesn't keep their word—get out of there. You have value. You will find another job. Don't stay in a situation that will prevent you from doing your best work. Don't trade your self-respect and your passion for a paycheck.

This, by the way, is what I mean when I say that real wealth is freedom. I always had the freedom to walk away from a job because I knew I had something of value that other people would pay for. I always knew another job was just around the corner. I also always had a side job, whether it was doing the books or managing an apartment building. We always had something coming in. That peace of mind—I'd say you can't buy it, but you can. You can buy it by living below your means, leveraging your skills into a part-time job, saving relentlessly, and investing (in my case, in real estate). I know I've said these things before, but they bear repeating here because you can see, can't you, how so many people stay in a situation like this because they believe they're stuck? Don't be stuck. Build your future now and have the freedom to walk when you need to.

Back to the things I did well, despite the situation. I left, as I mentioned, but I did something else that ended up working out very well for me. I agreed not to bad-mouth my former boss. He reached out to me and made the request, and I agreed. This wasn't just good for me professionally (he ended up recommending me for another job down the line), but it was good for me personally. It forced me to look at the situation and relationship in terms of what had gone well. He had mentored me, he had given me the opportunity to build a business from scratch, he had believed in me and funded the business. I had learned a lot from that experience. Instead of turning it into a personal issue or a feud between the two of us, I was able to see it as a learning experience and a tremendous personal success, one I would be able to parlay into every other business I started or worked in. These days we call it "spin," but I have to tell you, thinking about it in these terms made the entire experience ten times more valuable for me. So don't hold a grudge. It only detracts from your own life.

## Looking for Opportunities

I want to recap the idea of leveraging your skills:

- Know what you do very well. It can be tangible (writing contracts, auditing books, designing showrooms) or intangible (deep understanding of the local real estate market, the ability to connect people who need each other), but it should be something you excel at.
- Look for ways to trade skill for opportunity.
- Make sure there's something in it for you, even if the project never comes to fruition. And if it does see the light of day, make sure you're fairly compensated.
- Get the deal in writing.

Once you have an idea of what you can offer, start looking for ways to put it to use. If you don't already have a consulting side business that showcases your knowledge and abilities, start one. Put up a website, get cards made, make sure everyone knows you in terms of your particular expertise.

You can also look to relationships built while working your day job. Obviously, you don't want to do anything that's a conflict of interest, but consider what else might be possible. After I left government work, I ended up doing private accounting work for several of the people I had audited, because I was always scrupulously fair with them. I never created an antagonistic relationship; my point of view was always "If something is wrong, then this is what we need to do to fix it." Build your reputation on someone else's dime and get known for being both supremely competent and honorable.

Network, network, network. Throw a dinner party and invite friends who don't know each other but have common interests or compatible skills or business needs. Make sure they know that you're interested in projects where you can use your design/accounting/construction/PR skills. See if you can help someone in a small way that might lead to something bigger.

Once we start looking for something, opportunities abound. There's a point at which you'll have to say no, because every opportunity has a cost of time and energy, but you're probably not at that point yet. You build your leverage by building your skills and by investing in small opportunities that are a win-win for everyone involved.

Let me give you a couple of examples of small opportunities that became a win for everyone involved in them.

I'm an Italian American who likes to celebrate Italians, and the Italian American group I was involved with, the Italian Catholic Federation, needed a fundraiser to raise research funds for a blood disease, Cooley's anemia. I met a chocolate wholesaler who made chocolate eggs. Easter was coming up, there were 3,000 members in the federation in the state of California, and I figured, how hard could it be to sell each of them a chocolate egg? I purchased the eggs wholesale for $1.50 each and sold them for $3 apiece, with the profit going to the fundraiser. Let me lightly pass over the fact that 3,000 boxes of chocolate Easter eggs filled an entire bedroom; Bernice was not happy. So there was added incentive to sell some eggs.

And I did. I wrote a letter, which my talented brother Henry rewrote and vastly improved upon, and I went to every chapter in the state and I pushed those chocolate Easter eggs as the best possible way to celebrate the season. You were supporting a good cause, you were getting chocolate in the bargain, and if you had three kids, you definitely needed three of these eggs. I sold out. And we were able to make a large donation to important research, thanks to creativity and hustle (and to my wife being very understanding).

A few years later, when the Columbus Quincentenary was coming up in 1992, I wanted to find a book on Christopher Columbus for adult readers. And I couldn't find one. A friend of mine had an unpublished book on Columbus. Thanks to my experience with the Easter eggs, I knew I could make this book happen. I raised the money to get the book polished and published, and sold copies through a professional group as a fundraiser for them. Each chapter around the country sold the books, keeping $10 per book for each one sold.

Obviously, this was a win for my friend, whose book was finally in the hands of interested readers. It was a win for the organization, which benefited financially from book sales. And it was a win for me. It gave me a way to learn the nuts and bolts of publishing and selling a book with no financial risk to me. All of this laid the groundwork for my own digital-publishing nonprofit, The Mentoris Project. It also fulfilled my desire to help others. And it all came from seeing a need and being willing to jump in and do something about it.

Opportunities are everywhere. There is always something new to try and always something to get out of every experience, even the ones that don't turn out the way you planned.

## Vision and Value Creation

I am still not going to talk about leveraging your money. Of course you want your money to work for you, but there's a pretty thin line between investing money and gambling with it. I've made a lot on the stock market, but there have also been times when I've lost a lot. I don't want you to think that the only way to wealth is to throw everything into the latest market craze and hope for the best.

There is a better way, and that is creating value for others.

When you take something and make it better, not just for yourself but for other people in the world, you are leveraging your assets in a way that is absolutely unbeatable. When I started a leasing company, I didn't do what everyone else did—I did better. I saw a way to make leasing easier on the customers, and doing so made it far more profitable for us. When you look at a property to buy, you see the potential. When you realize that potential, that's when the money really starts to come in.

Do you understand? This is about vision. It's about building something great, not just something that's good enough. It is a philosophy that makes it easy to decide what to invest in and what not to invest in.

Don't buy at the top of the market.

Don't invest in a business that's already bringing in maximum profit.

Don't purchase a property that has nothing to improve on.

This is also a way to make money with integrity. It's not a winner-take-all game; you are always looking for something that benefits both of you. For instance, let's say you want to buy a franchise. Lots of people look for something that is a guaranteed moneymaker, but I don't. If the business has already reached its peak, then you purchasing it for top dollar is good for the seller, who maybe wants to start something new or retire to Italy. But it's not good for you. It means that you have no way to leverage that business to make more than what is already on the page. You are investing in something that can, at best, stagnate. Why would you pay for that? Equally, trying to squeeze someone out of a deal may be good (financially) for you, but it's unfair to them. And money is not worth as much as your reputation. You are always looking for a win-win.

This is where vision comes in. It is perfectly okay for you to give someone a fair price based on the current value of their business, and then pour time, money, energy, and creativity into taking that business up a notch or three once it's yours. They're happily touring around

Rome or Florence, and you're killing it here at home having doubled the business's revenue in two years. Everyone wins. Treat people fairly and they are more likely to be happy for your success.

Let's take property as an example, since that's what I know well. I'll talk in Chapter Eight about what to look for and what my own vision has always been, but for now, here's what you need to know.

Look for something that is not living up to its potential. There's no landscaping, the main door doesn't fully close, maybe some lights are out. The carpet is old, the paint is ugly, but it's structurally sound. It's in a good location. But it hasn't been given a lot of TLC.

Negotiate fairly with the owners for the property as it is now. I'm not saying pay the asking price; that's always just an opening gambit. But don't try to squeeze them so hard that there's no win in it for them. If the money is a little tight but you feel the value is there, think about what you can offer instead of money. There are lots of creative strategies for financing (again, Chapter Eight, I promise), but there are also intangibles that people need. They need a quick sale or a cash sale or sometimes they just want to know the place will be in good hands (this is truer with a home than with a complex). Whatever their situation, pay attention and see how you can meet those needs. You want the sale to be a win for both of you.

But remember that they are negotiating a fair price for the current property, as it is now. They are not negotiating with you for the property as it will be in five years, after you've invested time, sweat, and creativity. You don't have to share your plans with them. It's not wrong for you to make a profit, too. Both of you can win in this moment. Your success later doesn't take anything away from them.

Once you own the property, that's where your vision comes in. Now, you can upgrade the interior, put in landscaping (I'm a big fan of flowers), work with the tenants to make the place more desirable. This is where you make your real money. An apartment building that is already lovely and welcoming and getting top rent from a full slate of tenants—well, that's seductive. There's no work for you to do here, just maintain the status quo and count the money.

Do not be tempted.

There is no way to leverage that investment to be worth more. Yes, it's easier, but no, it will not build your wealth. Take something that has the potential to be top-notch (infrastructure and location being key), and put in the effort to upgrade the cosmetics of it, to address longstanding problems, to make the place so desirable that even existing tenants will be willing to pay more. That's where real money starts to come in. "Buy low, sell high" is the mantra of the stock market. Buy something that can be improved and then work hard to improve it— that's my real estate mantra.

This idea—envisioning a better product and working to bring that to life—can be mapped onto any investment. This is also where you get to be creative. Never look at something and say, "Well, everyone else is doing it this way" or "It's always been done this way," and believe that to be good enough. You can always find something to improve upon. Research. Ask questions. Ask the clients or the tenants what they would like to see or what their biggest hassles are. People love to give advice almost as much as they love to complain! Your job is to listen, look for the underlying problem, and fix it. That's what creates real value.

No matter what your investment is, never buy at the top of the market, no matter how tempting it is. Buy where there's potential, do your research, and create something that's better for you and for the world. Because in the long run, that is how you create a foundation of wealth.

# Investing

Ultimately, your investing strategy should be a three-legged stool:

1. Cash. This includes money and cash equivalents like savings, notes, bonds, annuities, and even life insurance.

2. Real Estate. You don't have to go all in with apartment complexes like I did, but you should own some property. Whether it's your own home or an income-generating property, you want to invest in a good place within a

growing community. Going for something with potential now means increasing your return on investment when the market catches up to it.

3. Business. This can be an investment in your own business or in other people's businesses. Again, when I talked about leveraging your talents for a stake in someone else's business, that's a good strategy. But you can also invest in other people's businesses directly by buying shares—and therefore ownership—in their companies.

# The Stock Market

Okay, so here's where I talk about investing your money rather than your talent. This is going to be boring. It should be boring. All that excitement I had day trading when I was young? Remember, that ended up in flames. My friends who gambled their paychecks have about as much to show for it as I do from that time. Here is the (boring) key to investing money in anything:

Have a long investment horizon.

You snoozing yet? I warned you. This is how to make money. And by long term here, I mean decades. If you need a million bucks by tomorrow, you need to win the lottery. And since you won't win the lottery, then tomorrow, instead of needing a million dollars, you'll need a million and one dollars because you'll be out the price of the ticket.

Getting rich quickly is a trap. Don't fall for it.

Getting rich slowly, however, is doable. Again, you want to look for value. It's tempting to buy the stock that's already prestigious because everyone is touting it, everyone is buying it, the price keeps going up, and you naturally want in on the action. But you don't want to buy something that has nowhere to go but down. As I developed a stock portfolio, I looked at blue chip stock for the long term and I invested in risk stock at a minimum. I observed the swings in stock investment, and the greatest growth came from long term. The Japanese have a mindset of long term that involves thinking in terms of generations. I

114

don't mean buy and hold for a generation, but buy something that you can grow for the long term, or that you can parlay into a long-term investment. No matter how old you are, think about what's in the best interest for everyone fifty years out. This is the way to build wealth.

Think about which stocks are going to improve over the next ten or twenty years, not which one will spike tomorrow. Sometimes this will mean taking a flier on something new and exciting that has the power to transform our lives, but most of the time it will be looking at what people need, what people will always need, and who provides that. And within that subsection, look for companies with vision and a commitment to excellence.

There it is, vision again. But this time, it's not your vision, it's the vision of the people running the company. You always want to be involved in projects where the leaders have a vision to improve things. (This, by the way, is a very different vision from someone who comes in with plans to make a quick profit and decimate the long-term viability of the business. It's important to recognize a long-term visionary over a short-term profit seeker.) Sometimes, a company with a vision will be one whose stock is already priced high. Go ahead, don't let me stop you from buying it. But be deliberate about it, and don't buy more of anything than you can afford to lose, especially not something that's already at a premium.

It's prudent to balance your investing goals, but to do that, you have to know what your investment goals are. You might think, well, I want to make money. That is not a useful goal. How much money? How quickly? For what purpose? More than once, we liquidated our stock portfolio to buy a building, but that's not the plan with my investments today. You also have to understand yourself. How much risk can you tolerate (not just to your portfolio, but for the sake of your health)? Don't just leap into the market without having a plan.

I am not going to tell you what to invest in; that would be foolish and instantly obsolete. What I will tell you is that stock market investment options are vast. Not just stocks and bonds, but mutual funds, emerging markets, common and preferred stocks . . . . As I write this, the market is going crazy over cryptocurrencies, something that wasn't even a word when I started investing. You need to educate yourself and then you need to see what people who succeed are doing, and evaluate for yourself what your best options are.

Let me underscore this point. The stock market is an arena where amateurs think they can make a killing. No one walks into an operating room thinking that watching medical shows on TV has made them capable of taking out someone's appendix, but plenty of people trade stocks just because they've watched the market go up and down. If you're going to invest your life savings—and I do NOT recommend that you start there—for heaven's sake, get educated first. Learn from experts. Make sure you understand how the market ticks. Take little steps to gain firsthand experience. Do not just throw money at stocks and assume you'll get rich.

So many people put their money into the stock market without any idea what to do next. They think it's a money machine and as long as they do what everyone else does, they'll make fast, easy money. No. If you do what everyone else does, you're part of the lemming herd. You must, at a minimum, understand how the market works and how the businesses you are investing in make their money—and the plans they have in place to continue to grow.

And you have to be prepared to sell. The market will go up, the market will go down. You have to be ready to get out and convert to cash—ideally, before it falls. You have to be educated and clear-eyed.

This is not easy, especially if you've been making money in stocks. When stocks go up and your money grows and grows—that's enticing. You don't want that to end, and there's a fear of missing out if you're wrong, if the stock continues to rise after you've sold. I understand. And you know what? It may keep going up, at least for a while. You may lose out on some gains. But pretending, when all the signs are there, that the stock market won't go down is like sticking your head in the sand and about as effective.

Remember that time I was on the board for a college that shall remain nameless? I was the only person on the board with financial experience. My specific role on the board was to help them grow their endowment. This was my "job," if you will, and I did it well. All of my recommendations were approved and we doubled their monies in just a few years.

Quick recap: I told them to sell. They refused. They lost all the gains we had made.

This was not my first rodeo. I could clearly see signs that the market was going to "correct," as the euphemism goes; it was definitely going down. Selling and waiting it out was the clear strategy. We had made more money than they could have hoped for; we just needed to bank it and wait for a better investing opportunity down the road. This was what I, the expert they had recruited, the one who had doubled their money, told them was a no-brainer decision.

And I was roundly voted down. By people who admitted they had done no research and knew nothing about the market. I talked about it earlier in this book in terms of how an understanding of numbers could have benefited them (not to mention listening to the actual expert). I mentioned then that I think part of the problem was that it wasn't their money, so there were no personal consequences to getting it wrong, whereas the status associated with making money for the college was high.

But there's something more going on here that I want you to look at: These people made a fear-based decision, pure and simple. The fear of missing out. Now, I'm not much for fear-based decisions in general. I'm the one with a wife and kids who walks out of a well-paying job with nothing on the horizon because it's the right thing to do. Imagine if fear had kept me in my first position decades ago? I'd still be working for the IRS, or maybe even decorating storefront windows. I certainly wouldn't be writing this book. So fear, for me, has no place in any important life decision.

But fear especially has no place in a monetary decision. This is what I mean when I tell you to have a long-term view. It's not just "buy and hold." It's looking at what the decision will have cost you twenty or thirty years from now. When you look at a market that has every sign of being about to crash, your options are:

1. Take out your money and protect your capital, or

2. Leave your money in the market.

Look dispassionately at the worst that could happen in either case. In the first case, although stocks may have gone up a few dollars while you were out of the game, your opportunity losses are not that great and your initial gains have been preserved. The market may stabilize. You can get back in it once the storm is over. Twenty years from now, those losses will have been a blip on your portfolio.

In the second case, the worst that can happen is you lose 50 percent or more of the value of your portfolio. That's what happened to the nameless college. You're going to waste the next ten years just getting back to where you were, and twenty years from now, you will still be far behind where you would have been had you not been afraid to sell.

I'm not going to tell you to try to time the market, because better people than you and me have tried and failed. What I am going to tell you to do is *pay attention*. Hedge your bets. Take a long-term view and don't let fear keep you from making good decisions.

Just as everyone wants to buy the "hot" stock, no one wants to risk putting money into the market after it crashes. But this is the best possible time to buy stocks that will increase in value. This is the kind of opportunity you look for. "Buy low and sell high" sounds simple, but you are fighting against human instinct—that lemming herd mentality—every time you do it. Be smart, be selective, be educated, and take a very long investment horizon. Think in terms of decades, and investing in the stock market can be a very good way to build your wealth.

# Equity

Think of equity in the same way. Long-term consideration is the way to build equity. Equity is this: It's the hidden value in what you already own. The obvious value of an apartment building, for instance, can be seen in the rent that the tenants currently pay, or in the market price for the building itself. But that's not equity. Equity is the value you have built up in the apartment building—or your house, or your business. It's threefold:

- What you own versus what you owe

- Potential
- Goodwill

First, what you own versus what you owe—this is Equity 101. If you buy a house for $100,000, put $50,000 down, and borrow the rest from the bank, your equity in the house is $50,000. What makes it more complicated is that the market value of your house can go both up and down. If the real estate market falls and your house can now only be sold for $75,000, your equity is only $25,000. But if home prices go up and your house is now valued at $200,000, you still only owe $50,000. Your equity in the house is now $150,000. This is of real value; it means you can borrow on that equity to invest in something else. I've done this over and over, parlaying equity in one property to purchase another, bigger one.

Potential is the second important aspect to building equity. When you buy a property, you need to have a vision for how it can be improved. Even if the real estate market remains flat, you can increase the value of your property—and therefore the equity you can tap into—by improving the property. Plus, landscaping, laying new carpet, or handling the top things that frustrate your tenants doesn't just increase the value of the property—it also attracts and retains tenants, and allows you to charge higher rents.

Finally, there's goodwill. You can't underestimate the value of having a good reputation, of treating people fairly. It's not about being "nice," it's about being fair. You always want to look for something that signals a win for everyone; never go into a negotiation thinking it's a zero-sum game. The strategy here is to find out what someone else wants and trade it for what you want so that everyone comes out happy.

One more thing about goodwill: Every so often, I see someone trade their integrity in order to beat someone else out in a deal. I just shake my head. They think they've won something, but they don't see that the cost of that small win has been tremendous. They've made enemies. They've revealed to peripheral players that they can't be trusted. Your reputation takes a lifetime to build and an instant to shatter, and the consequence will be fewer opportunities in the future.

Many people underestimate the value—the actual monetary value—of having a reputation for honesty and fairness. Don't you underestimate it, too. Your good name is the last thing you want to sacrifice.

Back to equity. I don't want you to think of equity just in terms of property. All of these things are true in a business as well. You've invested in your business, building equity in terms of the client list or the efficiency of the machines. You're also always working on the company's potential, fine-tuning your process, improving your product. You rise through your own efforts, never using other people to get ahead. Rather, you serve your clients, keep your word, and gain their trust and loyalty. You've built community goodwill, a superb product, and a well-oiled process, and you have ownership in the physical company. This is what builds equity in your business.

One other thing I have to tell you. I bought my last apartment complex before my first wife died. With Bernice gone, it would have been just a building, not a shared adventure. At that point, I no longer needed to leverage one building to buy another. I carried a total debt of $21 million, and within just a few years, I had paid it off completely. I paid off high-interest loans first, sometimes borrowing more money at a lower interest rate to pay them, then I paid off everything else. I really devoted all of my energy into clearing that debt so that everything was equity. I did this for my family, but I also did it for myself. Debt is a burden—a useful burden when you're building your business. But there comes a time when you've built enough. At that point, equity is everything.

# Appreciation

There are different ways things can increase in value. The desire for it can go up, increasing its potential sales price. This is what happens when you buy a home, your neighborhood improves, people want to move there, and suddenly houses on your street are selling for twice what you paid for yours. Your home has appreciated in value.

But that doesn't mean that money is in your pocket. To realize the appreciation in value, you would have to sell the house and find somewhere else to live. The downside, of course, is that the market has probably gone up in more than just your neighborhood and buying a comparable home will cost you the same as—or more than—the sales price of your own house. At the end of the day, you still have the same amount in your savings account; you have just swapped one house for another.

The real value of a home's appreciation is in the equity it unlocks. Let's keep the numbers simple and say you bought your house for $100,000. You put some money down, you've paid off part of your mortgage, and now the balance on the mortgage is $60,000. Your equity in the house is $40,000.

But then you realize the house has appreciated. Now on the open market it would sell for $200,000. Your mortgage balance is still $60,000, but your equity is $140,000. That's money you can leverage to buy a rental property or a clothing factory or whatever else would expand your business. Be smart; you don't want to stretch yourself so thin that your family winds up on the street, but growing your business is a more financially prudent use of your home's equity then, say, remodeling the bathroom. You can live with the ugly tile a little longer.

There are other investments that appreciate; they may go up and down in the short term, but over the long haul, the price will increase faster than the pace of inflation. Think of paintings, gold, antiques . . . anything with the potential to be worth more tomorrow than it is today. There's that word *potential* again. Buying something that's already at the top of its price range isn't a smart investment. You buy a new car because you want a new car, not because you hope to sell it for more in five or ten years. Know the difference.

## When Things Go Down

You must go into every business understanding that there are good times and there are bad times. Being flexible has allowed me to move from one industry to another and one investment strategy to another as the economy stalls in one area or grows in another. But that doesn't mean I'm impervious to an economic downturn. For one thing, my income from the apartment buildings is dependent on people being able to pay rent. If they lose their jobs, I lose my tenants and I can't fill my vacancies. I make sure I provide above-average housing at fair market prices—I don't gouge—but if the economy tanks, well, we're all in this together.

You need a cushion. I never moved on anything without having a worst-case scenario in place. We could always sell the house and move into one of our own units. I didn't want to do that—that was definitely not Plan A or even Plan B—but it was a safety net. I never did anything without a safety net. Could I have made more money with a higher tolerance for risk? Maybe. But I don't need more money; what I did need was the peace of mind knowing that my family would be taken care of. It's just like insurance. Hedging your bets lowers your risk and keeps everyone safe when things go wrong—which they will. Be smart. Be prepared.

# Gratitude

I want to talk about another kind of appreciation. Don't be stingy with gratitude. Valuing other people for their contribution to your life creates that goodwill I was talking about. It also creates a team spirit: "We did it together!"

I said it earlier, but let me reiterate here: You can't do everything all by yourself. You need to cultivate relationships to find the people you want to work with at every step of your career. You need people you can trust and who share your values and your vision. You also need to learn how to manage those people.

Managing is one of those "soft" skills that doesn't necessarily translate directly into income, but can save you thousands of dollars over time. You want to retain good people and that means making them feel valued and respected.

To do that, you have to be willing to listen with an open mind. Everyone looks at a situation from a different perspective. Think of my kids going through a building for us to invest in. One of them looks at the roof, one of them interviews a tenant, one of them gets in there and finds out about the plumbing. When we meet up for them to give me reports, they each have a different perspective about the potential value of the investment. And they are all in the right, even when they disagree with each other and with me. They are 100 percent from their own standpoint, because each one is an expert on one thing. It's up to me to listen to them, take in all the information, and decide what matters most. Major structural problem? Then I don't care how stable the tenants are or how new the pipes. The key is not to make anyone feel as if their perspective is wrong or is being dismissed out of hand. Ultimately, the decision is yours, but listening, listening—that's the key. Listen for the options other people present with an open mind and let them know their input is valuable even if you decide to go another way.

You don't want people around you who always agree with you. If that's what you need to prop up your ego, let me tell you, it is the quickest way to making terrible decisions that could cost you everything. A smart businessperson wants to be surrounded by clear-eyed experts who aren't afraid to tell you that you're nuts.

My children and grandchildren are good at that.

And I'm grateful that they are. When they questioned me about doing an investment in the current market, I didn't take it personally. They're doing me a favor: They are forcing me to articulate my reasoning. If there's a flaw in it, they'll find it. I make million-dollar deals. If I ran around going on "gut instinct," well, that would just be my ego running wild. I'm a businessperson, not a psychic. Surround yourself with people who will keep you on your toes, who will give you expert advice in their own field.

Appreciate them.

## Buying and Selling

I talk about negotiating as a win-win. Buying and selling products is just another form of negotiation, and once again, I'm going to push for a win-win here. If you're selling something and it's not going to enhance the purchaser's life, why are you selling it? Don't sell something you don't believe in. Make it valuable, whether it's insurance or homemade shampoo or diamonds.

In fact, let me talk about those diamonds for a second.

Diamonds are one of those things that, for the most part, are not really useful. Most of the people who buy them don't plan to use them for anything other than as an adornment. They're pretty, but to me they're not as pretty as other gemstones, and the synthetic ones are darn good ringers these days. What is all the fuss about? And yet every day, people pay top dollar for real diamonds.

This, to me, is why diamonds are a perfect example of how to create a win-win. If all you're looking at is a monetary transaction, then no one really makes money on diamonds. You buy a diamond worth $1,000 for $1,000. The person parts with a $1,000 diamond for $1,000. Where's the win here?

The answer is that money is not the real object of a diamond purchase. The win here is not that you're making an investment that you can resell at a profit. Diamonds are symbols. The win for the buyer isn't how much money they'll make, but how they'll feel, the psychological value of buying and wearing the diamond.

It's not wrong to give the buyer a fantastic experience. That is what they want, that is what they're buying. In fact, they will be *happier* if you fulfill their psychological needs than if you give them a bargain on the stone. The stone may represent eternal love (engagement ring) or that someone has reached the top of their game (Super Bowl ring). In neither case would the experience be enhanced by talking about what a bargain they got on the diamonds!

Whatever you're buying or selling, you need to start by knowing the market price. If you're the buyer, think about what you really want from the deal; what, for you, is the win? You should expect that the first offer will have a cushion; the seller will expect you to counter at a lower price. But here is also where you have to think about the seller's needs. What do they really want? Do they need a quick sale, a cash offer, the feeling that their home/heirloom/artwork is going to be loved and appreciated? I know someone who bought a baritone horn amid multiple offers because her son would actually play it, while the other offers wanted it for restaurant decor. Meeting the seller's psychological needs is just as important as meeting their business needs, and more important than meeting their initial asking price.

If you're the seller, this is all true for you as well. You want to create an experience for the buyer, not just throw a thing at them and ask for money in return. Think of all the effort that goes into staging homes, even to the point of baking fresh cookies so the house smells like childhood memories. This isn't deceptive—you can actually bake cookies once you buy the house. What it does is vividly bring out the potential of the purchase. It meets the psychological needs of a home buyer.

If you're selling, you also need to know the tax implications of the sale, be prepared for a counteroffer, and know what really matters to you. Be willing to give on the things that don't matter, but don't compromise what you need from the sale.

Whether you're buying or selling, be honest in your dealings and try to make the experience a good one for the people on the other side of the table. In fact, never think of it as being on one side with them on the other. When I was auditing businesses for the government, I never sat across from someone, but next to them. We were working out the problems together. That philosophy is the basis of every successful negotiation.

## Leveraging Other People's Money

Other People's Money (known as OPM) is the best way to leverage your own funds and skills. The kinds of deals I just told you about, where your direct investment isn't money but skills or the ability to put people together to get the deal done, those are essentially OPM opportunities. You are leveraging your abilities and other people are funding the project.

There are other ways to tap into OPM. With a loan, you're using OPM—from partners, investors, banks, or credit unions—to invest in property or your business. In Chapter Eight, when I talk about investing in real estate, I'll go over the idea of having the seller take out a junior loan, or a second loan on the same property after the mortgage loan, which is often very attractive to them because they'll be making interest on what had been their own property or business.

Your first foray will largely be with your own money. Maybe you can get your family to help you out if you need it. But partners, banks, investors—they're unlikely to be willing to step in if you don't have a track record. Your first big investment is your proving ground, and you need to sacrifice, sometimes for years, to build up enough of a base that you are ready when the right business or property or investment comes around. And then you sacrifice by putting your all into it for as long as it takes to be a success. Everyone wants to back a winner, and once you've proven yourself, OPM will start to flow.

And then you do it all over again.

## A Quick Word on Taxes

Paying taxes is like having a silent partner—one we can't be without. The government provides us safety, infrastructure, and social programs. Tax laws are complicated not just because there are so many contingencies to plan for, but because taxes are used to discourage some behaviors (like smoking) and encourage others (like home ownership or drilling for oil). It's incumbent upon you to pay your taxes, but also to understand the tax breaks available to you if you conduct your business a certain way. Get educated and get someone who really understands the tax code to help you make sense of it and stay compliant.

Too many people make the mistake of making a financial decision because of a tax break, such as going into a particular business for a tax write-off, or even making certain donations to charity. Make sure you really understand the implications of your decisions. If you want to donate to a charity or go into business for other reasons, of course you should do so. But doing it strictly for supposed tax benefits almost never makes good financial sense in the long run.

# Striking Out on Your Own

One of the most important things Bernice ever said to me was "When are you going to stop making money for someone else and start making it for us?" She wasn't talking about earning a paycheck; she was talking about creating value. I created tremendous value for customers—and so for the company I worked for—in leasing cars, in managing a restaurant, and in running a credit union. That added value filled each company's coffers, but none of those companies were mine (even with the restaurant, my stake was in the land, not the business). I don't regret the hard work I did, mind you, because each situation was a learning opportunity, a chance to test myself on someone else's nickel. But Bernice was right. At some point, I needed to act. I needed to make money for us, which meant striking out on my own and working for myself.

Here is the very best advice I can give you:

- Learn the basic skills you need while someone else is paying you.
- Test the waters with a side business so you can make your rookie mistakes before your family's well-being is at stake.
- When you go for it, go for it fully. See your idea through.

Does this sound too easy? It's simple, I will grant you, but it's not easy. I've known a lot of people who listen to me and say "I already knew that," but the thing they're not seeing is that they may know it, but they're not acting on it.

Some people get hit with bad luck. Some people live in places where there are few opportunities. Some people have major family responsibilities, like caregiving for a parent, that fill all of their available time and energy. I'm not suggesting that you can succeed at launching a business every time you try, or at every stage of your life, with just a can-do attitude. But I am telling you that the three pieces of advice I just mentioned provide a foundation that improves your rate of success. And no matter where you are in life, what circumstances surround you, you can probably incorporate one of these three things. Keep your eyes and ears open and learn how your boss handles the bookkeeping and the marketing and managing the staff. See if you can move laterally within your company to learn something new. Stuck in a small town? The Internet opens you up to a wider world. Research a small side business where you can test your business idea as well as your skills. You don't have to leap right to "quit your day job." You shouldn't.

But when you do, be bold.

To succeed in a big way, you need to be unrelenting. You need drive, you need focus, and you need a plan with clear next steps that may seem a little frightening. But you're going to take those steps anyway. A plan can't just be "Well, I hope this will happen." It is a series of steps you will take to tilt the odds of good things happening in your favor. They are clear, they are actionable, and they have deadlines attached. Keep track of everything so you can see what works and what doesn't, and double down on the things that work. If it doesn't look like a daunting amount of hard work, it's probably not a good plan, because if it were easy, you—or someone else—would already have done it.

People have no scarcity of good ideas. What they usually lack are persistence and a willingness to roll up their sleeves and do the hard work.

Also, you're going to fail. Have you heard the saying "Nobody plans to fail, they just fail to plan?" I'm telling you, you need to plan what you will do if you fail. You need to build that into your strategy, because if you don't, you'll never have the mindset needed to rebuild when things go wrong.

It is very important when you are creating your plan that you look at the worst-case scenario. The worst case for my family, when I sunk everything into that first apartment complex, was that we would have to sell our house and move into one of the apartments. It wouldn't have been ideal, but we would have had a roof over our heads. It didn't happen, but if it had, it would have been a setback we could weather. My parents lost everything not once, but twice. Each time, they rebuilt, both together and separately. This is what I mean when I say "relentless."

Hedge your bets with insurance (never go without appropriate insurance!), have a plan in place so that you don't panic if the worst happens, and then commit fully to success. Things will go wrong, and whether they were outside your control or something you could have prevented, it doesn't matter. Learn from them, but don't dwell on them.

Revisit your business plan. See what you need to do differently. Start over. Do it all again.

When you work for someone else, you will (I hope) be providing value to your employer, their customers, and their business. Essentially, you are building equity for them in their business by making it more successful and therefore more valuable. When you work for yourself, you need to think about how to build equity in your own company.

Think about this for a minute: It is not just about doing a good job for your clients or building a better thingamabob. It is about making choices that add value to your business beyond your direct involvement. Streamlining your process, upgrading equipment, building a deep client base, and solving recurring problems all add value to the overall business as well as improving your profit margins.

Sit down and write out all the ways in which your company could become more profitable and more productive. How can it better serve your clients and your community? How can it be more efficient? You don't have to come up with solutions here, you just need to be able to identify the areas where improvement is possible. Seeing the hole is the first step to filling it. When you have a list, start thinking about who works directly in each arena. Who would have firsthand knowledge of the problem and might even have some ideas for solutions? So many managers come in and lay down a solution by decree without talking to the people who would have to implement it. This isn't even a rookie mistake, it's an ego problem. It's dividing the world into "little people" who do what they're told and corporate VIPs who have all the answers. It's a trap. Don't fall into it.

When we're considering buying an apartment complex, one of the first things we do is talk to the tenants. That's right, we actually go door to door and talk to the people who are living in the building. We ask them what works, what doesn't, and what ideas they have for improvements. What a concept—actually seeking input from the people with the most direct experience and who have the most at stake!

No matter what business you're in, there are people who can help you add value if only you would seek them out.

Your ultimate goal should be to be able to take yourself out of the company and have it remain successful. This is why I train my children and my grandchildren to take over from me, but also why I train my managers and only hire people I respect. You want to create a culture that respects your employees and your clients and encourages everyone on the team to add value as well. Embrace good ideas, no matter where they come from. Promote people who demonstrate capability and creativity. Create a self-reinforcing cycle of contribution and improvement. Rather than complain that you have to do everything yourself, take the time—take the responsibility—to lay the groundwork that allows others to contribute fully to your vision. That is perhaps the greatest value you can add to your business.

# RECAP: POWER EARNING

- **Leverage your unique skills and contribution.** Be clear on what you and only you (and your company) can provide and look for ways to trade that expertise for a partnership or stake.

- **Get all agreements in writing.** If you follow no other advice in this book, follow this one.

- **Purchase potential, not bragging rights.**

- **Have a long investment horizon.** Get rich slowly. Start small and learn as you go. Don't let greed or fear keep you from making well-reasoned decisions.

- **What goes up will also go down.** Be prepared to pivot.

- **Successful buying and selling is the art of making both parties feel that they have negotiated a win.**

- **Add value to your business and create a company culture where others are encouraged to add value as well.**

# CHAPTER EIGHT

## INVESTING IN REAL ESTATE

Real estate is how my mother made her money, and how Bernice and I primarily made ours. If there's anything I'm a real cheerleader for, it's buying real estate. Not houses, not duplexes, but apartment complexes. The opportunity to bring value to and make money with multiple-unit properties is immense.

So are the pitfalls.

I have several friends who have watched me succeed at owning and managing apartment buildings. Four of them asked for my help choosing buildings or evaluating ones they've already purchased so that they could also succeed. All of them ended up selling out after only a couple of years.

I need to do some disclaiming before we move into this chapter. I am a guy who has made a lot of money and lived a full and happy life. I am writing this book in the hopes that you, too, will make a lot of money and live a full and happy life. I am not telling you exactly what to buy, invest in, rent, sell, or otherwise do. How could I? Your life, your personality, your circumstances, and your dreams are all your own. In addition, it would be an impossible task to teach you all you need to know about anything financial in just one book. I majored in accounting and spent a lifetime reading contracts and auditing books; you need at minimum to do some independent research. I do advocate learning by doing, but for crying out loud, start out with low stakes. Don't buy the next apartment complex you see for sale and complain that Barbera told you to do it.

Get educated, make your own decisions, and don't blame me.

In this chapter, I will point you in a lot of directions where investment money may lurk, where good property may be waiting, and where creative funding can make a big difference. But I will also say that owning and managing apartments is not for everyone. It is a lot more work than you think it will be. If you're going to maximize your profits, you have to maximize your own direct involvement—and maybe even live there yourself. You need to dive into contracts, research local neighborhoods, build a great support team, learn how to collect rents, and be relentless about creating value for your tenants.

## Have a Plan

You are not going to buy a building just to say you own a building. That's ridiculous. We looked for over two years before we found our first property. And even before that, we had a plan in place. I established a company with a purpose: to develop the apartments we owned to their highest and best use. That was always the vision. It was never about flipping properties or stripping them of their resources, but about developing them, nurturing them. I wanted to own places that tenants wanted to live in, and I always started with someplace that had room for improvement. That was always the plan.

No building we ever purchased was at its peak for maximum rent schedules. There was always room to go up, and we would start by tackling the things that mattered most to tenants. That almost always meant updating the kitchens and bathrooms. Our building may not have been the newest on the block, but you wouldn't be able to tell by the amenities. We took out trees to prevent damage to plumbing lines and foundations, we added flowers, we installed watering systems on the grounds that used minimal water for maximum results and to save on natural resources. We enhanced the style of each building inside and out, and we created a unique feeling when you walked onto the property; this played into our marketing as well, as we gave each property a special name to distinguish it from neighboring buildings.

None of this was by accident. Sure, some things we learned from early mistakes, but the concept, the vision, the idea that we would take run-of-the-mill properties and transform them into living spaces that were unique and top-tier—that was always the vision.

## Location, Location, Location

This catchphrase doesn't mean what you think it means.

For most people, "location" means looking for a place that is already booming: great schools, lots of foot traffic, a neighborhood that is already desirable. Already at a premium.

I'm going to be blunt here: That is a very stupid way to invest.

You don't want to invest in a neighborhood that is already at the top of its potential. There is nowhere to go but down. There's one neighborhood near me—I won't mention which one—but I wouldn't buy property there in a million years. It's a very expensive area and the people who want to live there are very demanding. They would make difficult tenants and I don't need that kind of hassle.

You also don't want to invest in a crime-ridden, high-unemployment area without the social scaffolding necessary for it to improve. I don't like dead ends, noisy traffic, or industrial areas. What you're really looking for is a property in a modest neighborhood with great growth potential. Where's the business district? In which direction is it growing out; where is it spreading to? Buy a building in a neighborhood that is going to become a hub, not one that already is.

## Red Flags

Beyond location issues and the property already being at the top of its potential, there are other things that are deal breakers for me when I'm looking at a building. One is sunlight. If the building is murky, that's already one strike, but if you have apartments in it that get little to no light, definitely walk away. Those are dead units. You'll never be able to get top rates for them, if you can lease them at all, and when you do lease them, you'll have more turnover than you want. I don't want to live in the dark, so why would my tenants? Natural light is a big deal.

Don't just look at the deal as it exists "on paper." Your visit to the property isn't a formality, it's an investigation. You're the detective and you have to ferret out all the things that are wrong. I turned down a building because the bathrooms only had fans, no windows, and the humidity in them was depressing. One guy I knew wanted to buy an apartment building that had nineteen units, but only sixteen parking spaces. Those last three units were going to be impossible to rent, at least for top dollar, in a place like Los Angeles where people need cars to get anywhere. Spend time at the building. Count the parking spaces, ask tenants what bugs them—oh, and make sure to check with the tenants once you're given a rent schedule that they do pay what the seller says, and they have lived there as long as it's been reported. It's one thing to present a property in a flattering light; it's quite another to falsify records. A big red flag is getting involved with a seller who is that unethical.

Other problems with the building itself can include costly maintenance that the former owner had deferred. If you need a new roof right away, that's a problem. Your discretionary funds are going to be tied up in the purchase price, so you may have to end up pushing off that new roof yourself, and that's the kind of problem that can come back to bite you. I looked for places that were undervalued, where I could make capital improvements that would make a big difference and pay off relatively quickly (within three years). That is a very different proposition from having to shore up bad plumbing or put in a new furnace; people expect heat and running water as a given—it's not a premium feature you can charge more for. Finally, if the building is rent-controlled, none of your improvements will see an adequate return on investment. These are all things to keep in mind.

I also don't want to buy property that is too far for me to be able to visit it. That's not as wide an area as you think. Of course it's a mistake to purchase property in another state, but even within my own county, distance can be challenging. Ideally (and it took years, but this is what we have now) you want your properties on a circuit so that your maintenance company, your landscaping people, your employees—and, of course, you—can reach them all easily.

Sometimes a red flag will pop up for someone else and threaten your ability to make the purchase. One Saturday night, I got a call from the bank—and yes, my banker was actually working late on a Saturday night. He was very worried about my pending loan.

"Barbera," he told me, "I want to give you this loan. You have this wonderful record, you always pay on time, I want to say yes, but have you seen the property you're buying? It's two blocks from another property we're foreclosing on. Are you sure about this neighborhood?"

If I hadn't been vigilant, I might have been worried, too. But I knew the neighborhood. Plus, I'm from New York. When I lived in the city, I would walk to work every morning on Third Street, passing a bar on every corner and stepping over drunks where I had to. Three blocks away was Park Avenue, the most expensive piece of real estate you could buy. From the absurd to the ridiculous in only three blocks.

And that's what I told him. I explained not only the difference between the two neighborhoods in question, but that I'd also looked at the building he was foreclosing on when it had been up for sale a couple of years earlier. It was a terrible property! A three-story building with a rickety elevator continually breaking down, plus three units on every floor that are enclosed with no sunlight. Dead units, ones you'll never be able to rent. I was able to spell out why the bank would foreclose on that one, and why I'd be making money for years on the other. And he gave me the loan. Being attuned to red flags can tell you when to run, but it can also help you convince someone to back your horse over another.

## Creating Value

I credit my son, John, who has a critical eye, when it comes to paying attention to the details on the outside of our properties. Most of us get used to and accept the appearance of our properties, but not John. Maintenance is crucial. I keep every property as if it will go up for sale tomorrow. That means no deferred maintenance, no peeled paint, no cracked walls. Inside, we install the most current, modern fixtures, including toilets that use the least amount of water. I have a couple of personal preferences that I always put in. One is that we rip up the carpets from the dining rooms and install tile, which looks very sharp and sets our properties apart visually from others. The other is that on the outside, we have flowers. If a bush doesn't flower, I don't want it on my site. I also take out trees; they're expensive to maintain and can potentially cause damage. Inside and outside, we keep everything looking beautiful and, as I mentioned earlier, unique.

Keeping the maintenance up to date doesn't just create value; it actually costs us less to maintain the property if we catch everything early and fix it right away. Also, tenants are more comfortable, more likely to stay, and more likely to treat the property with the respect it deserves. Once you start letting things slide, other people will as well.

# Negotiating

Negotiating the purchase or sale price of property is critical, whichever side of the table you're on. On one hand, I am always willing to walk away from a bad deal—which, to me, could mean a number of things. It could mean they're unwilling to wiggle on the price and I feel it's overvalued, or it could mean the other party is hard to get along with or their ego or need for power is engaged. Who wants that kind of hassle? No one building will make or break my business; walking away is always an option.

On the other hand, it is critical to me to create a win-win. I don't want a one-sided negotiation. If I were to force someone into a bad deal to get something I didn't deserve, that would weigh on my conscience.

Know what you want from the negotiation, be it price or creative financing or something else, tangible or intangible, that really matters to you. Set your top price—don't tell them what it is, mind you, but set it in stone for yourself—so that you don't get caught up in the bidding-war mentality.

One time, when an estate sale was available, I made the first offer with the allowable 10 percent reduction. At the time of the court appearance, anyone could offer the original price, which meant I had to bid up from the new offer—this was a possibility I had anticipated, and while I would have preferred them to take my initial offer, I had finances in place to go up a certain amount. I also had a maximum offer that I was willing to make, and quite simply, I was outbid. This happens. I didn't let my ego push my bid beyond what I could afford. But the people who outbid me, well, they had let their desire for the property outstrip their ability to pay for it. Two months later, they realized they could not sustain their offer and gave me the option to buy the property at my price. The moral of the story is this: Give yourself limits and stick to them; don't let emotion carry you away.

Remember that any time someone is selling a property, it's because they are trying to get rid of it. They will tell you why, and what they tell you might or might not be the whole truth. Of course they're going to shine the best possible light on the property, so it's up to you to stay rational and do your due diligence. But it also means that they're going to be happy to sell. They don't begrudge you the chance to make money. The key is to really look for the real, underlying reason they're selling, because if you can give them what they truly want from the sale, your offer becomes that much more attractive to them.

Another thing I'll just mention as an aside: I always found the heirs to a property to be easier to negotiate with than the owners. With owners, there is a deeper understanding of the value of the property, and there may also be emotional baggage: They may be selling to move onto an exciting new adventure, which is great—or, on the other hand, they may be selling from a sense of defeat that they didn't succeed as well as they'd hoped. Keep in mind that what they really want may not be the money, but the validation that comes from "beating you" in the negotiation. That's a hard place from which to create a mutual win.

The first price mentioned by any seller is just the opening salvo; no one expects you to meet the asking price right away. One key component, however, is to figure out what their real price is and also who set it for them. Remember, you're buying a property that is not at its top earning potential; they're selling that property, the not-top one, not the one you envision. Their asking price should reflect the reality that this property requires work to bring it up to your standards. You can meet a fair price for them and still make money if you can unlock the potential in the building—and if you can't, you shouldn't be buying it.

Having a trusted real estate broker, and ideally one who knows all the players, is critical. The more they understand what everyone's real goal is—to get quick cash, to get the best possible price to fund their retirement, to never have to talk to their sibling again (don't laugh, this happens with heirs who don't like each other)—the better your chances of a fair and easy negotiation.

When I walk into a negotiation, I usually already have some good relationships going. I work with the same real estate broker all the time, I know the people at the bank, I try to develop a good rapport with everyone. I never walk in with the idea that I will get one over on someone. Yes, I have a vision for their property that they don't have, but they don't want my vision, they want my money! I've been on the sales side of the table, too, sometimes with a property that I despaired of selling in time to buy a better one that was in my sights. I am happy for the buyer to make money where I couldn't, or where I no longer wanted to. A successful negotiation is all about meeting the needs of everyone wherever they are in their lives right now.

Something I didn't mention earlier when I was talking about relationships is that a face-to-face meeting will always be better than any other interaction. I don't mail something or e-mail it; I don't even pick up the phone if I can go down to your office and spend ten minutes talking to you in person instead. There are those who will say that's not efficient, just send an e-mail, I'm wasting my time. I'm telling you the opposite. Handling a problem in person takes away all the possible miscommunication that can come from an e-mail or a phone call while at the same time allowing you to build a relationship. It is tremendously efficient, and it can turn what would be faceless names into friends who are eager to help you out in a pinch.

Sometimes, of course, you will be the seller and not the buyer. All of the above still holds true. You need to be able to evaluate the market price of your property. You need to know how far down you are willing to go before walking away, and to understand what you need from the sale beyond the best price. You need to know the financing you expect to see—will it be you who is asked to take back a note?—and you must, must, must understand the tax implications. All of this is critical to your success.

## Getting the Money Together

We are afloat with cash. Cash is all around us. We just need a way to pull it together.

You have to start with your own savings. While Other People's Money sounds great (and trust me, it is great), the foundation for getting to use OPM is putting YOM—Your Own Money—out there and showing what you can do with it.

- Save day by day to build a nest egg. Do without and learn to love a bargain until you are able to stash away from a third to half of your income.
- Cut your budget and remove unnecessary things from your life. This takes creativity. I'm not asking you to live in a garret, I'm saying build a life you enjoy that doesn't cost you as much as it does now.
- Move into small investments and savings accounts to start earning interest and dividends.
- Do outstanding work at your day job. Get raises. Put those raises directly into your savings account.
- Have a part-time job or side business to bring in extra money and build your investment fund that much faster.
- Cut up your credit cards.

When you can prove you know how to build your savings, when you show that you have money to invest and that you know what to do with it when you do invest, then you can convince people to let you work with their money as well. This is where all your relationships come in:

- Join with others to invest, stretching your funds.

139

- Develop lines of credit with banks. Meet bankers, get to know them personally, develop lines of credit before you need the cash. Meet every commitment early on, because there will come a moment when you can't meet a commitment, when you need an extension, and you need to have a track record to point to so that they know you can be trusted a little longer.
- Develop a reputation for know-how.
- Stay close to people with cash.

You can get cash if people think you know what you're doing. If your need fills a market, you can make good use of their loan money. Most people want you to succeed for them—it's less work on their part. If you build from success in increments, money will come to you. You take the first risk with your nest egg.

Putting a deal together takes some creativity.

You also need an asset base that is lendable to cover a loan. Each of these is beyond the scope of this book; that's what classes and mentors are for. Educate yourself. But let me point you to some options:

- Consider stock margin.
- Get a loan on an insurance policy.
- Get an equity loan on existing real estate. I leveraged every real estate purchase I made as soon as there was equity to be used.
- Convince other people to lend you their money at good rates.

That last one is not as hard as you think it is. You might be able to borrow from your family; just be sure to pay them back promptly. Money can rip families apart, and I don't want that to happen to you. But you can also borrow from complete strangers. Here's an example: I had a friend who was a lawyer; he had a client with over $100,000 in cash with no experience who wanted to invest the money. I made a deal to borrow the money under a good arrangement to use it to buy a property. The investor made back steady interest from me, and I made money on the appreciation of the property.

Twice, I bought foreclosed property from the bank with nothing down. Both times, I was able to improve the property and sell it for more than I owed. The bank was thrilled not to have the properties on their books anymore, and I had a way into ownership with no money down. Look for people who want to be in on something without the knowledge (my friend's client) or time (the bank) to do the work themselves. If there is already a note on the property, see if that original holder is willing to keep it; often they are, because they're getting a good interest rate and/or because of the tax implications if that note is suddenly paid for. When you offer someone a solution that helps them make money, or when you bring the expertise, the bird-dogging, the sweat equity to the table, that's when you can make a deal.

Sometimes you have to be creative. There was one apartment building I wanted and Bernice ran the numbers.

"You don't have the money to buy the building," she told me.

"Watch me," I said.

"You don't have it," Bernice repeated.

"Sit tight," I told her.

I went to two of my existing tenants (both of whom I knew personally and who had some disposable income) and told them that I would give them 10 percent off their rent if they paid a year's rent in advance. Ten percent was far more than that money was making sitting in their savings accounts; it was a great return for them, and I framed it as "How would you like to pay less rent?" Who wouldn't want to take that deal? And it gave me the extra capital I needed to make the deal I wanted to make.

When you look closely at each of these examples, you'll see I was able to make these deals because of contacts, relationships. People say it's not what you know, it's who you know; that's true, but it's not nearly as cynical as it sounds. Neither of these examples was a case of me knowing the right people; each time, it was a case of the right people knowing *me*. Knowing I was a man of integrity, knowing I was good at what I did, knowing that I understood the real estate market. If I said there was money to be made in a building, I was usually right. And I never left a partner holding the bag.

Having a nest egg is essential, but having a stellar reputation—that's critical. That's the foundation on which you build. Make contacts not just so you'll know who can help you, but so they'll know that you can help them.

Finally, most purchases are made with the seller taking back a note. Sometimes you can even get the realtor to take back a junior loan in lieu of their commission. In this way you minimize the cash needed for purchase. But there's an additional advantage to having the seller take a note: When they first do it, they're usually delighted. It means they are still earning income (the interest) on what had been their property, but with no work involved. It's passive income, and it's what they want at the time of sale. But people's lives change, their needs change. Sooner or later (and it's usually sooner), the cash represented by the note becomes more tempting to them than the interest they're earning. They will want to turn their note into cash immediately, which means they have to sell at a discount. The discount can be anything from 20 percent to 50 percent. By then, I have my credit line back up and sufficient to buy the second trust deed. They get the cash, and I get the second trust deed for the credit line rate, which will inevitably be lower than the original interest rate I was paying.

## Second Trust Deeds

Let me talk for a second about second trust deeds. Teaching you how to effectively buy and sell trust deeds is, again, beyond the scope of this book. In short, in the context of buying property, the first deed on the house is the original mortgage (usually from a bank, sometimes from an individual owner or builder), and the second deed is either a second mortgage from another bank or a loan from the seller or other individual with the house again as collateral. You pay back principal and interest on these deeds just like you pay a mortgage, and you structure it so that the deeds don't come due until you have positive cash flow. Sometimes, as I mentioned above, you can buy them back early at a discount or renegotiate for a better rate. They can often give you the wiggle room you need to put together a winning financing deal.

For one of our buildings, one we really had to stretch to afford, there were six owners, all of whom had an interest in the property. All of them were doctors with sufficient savings to take back trust deeds. We set up six trust deeds, all falling due in sequence, and we used the rent we collected to pay them off one by one. As long as you make sure you'll have the income coming in to pay them off, trust deeds can be a terrific way to leverage other people's money.

## CASE STUDY

## How Longden was Purchased

Let me tell you about a specific purchase and the improvements we made on it so that you can see an example of how everything unfolds. This is one of my favorite examples because of all the elements that came into play to acquire the building in Temple City, California, including timing, negotiation, leverage, and luck.

Actually, before I talk about Longden itself, you need to know about the property I bought before it, and its sale. The earlier property was in Whittier, California. It was a sixteen-unit apartment house that we purchased with a typical 20 percent down payment; in this case, of $50,000. The previous owner—the one who sold it to us—took back 80 percent of the first trust deed, so our "mortgage" on it was with the owner, not a bank. That seller felt the interest on holding such a large trust deed was a good investment for their retirement. In fact, it was a great deal for them because they would actually be making a little more from their note than they had been getting for actually running the building. I, of course, was set to create more value. So the Whittier property was a win for everyone.

In terms of return on our investment, we weren't

wrong. Over the next two years, the property produced the usual expected ROI; financially, everything was great. But the property also took more management work than we had expected. For one thing, this was before I realized how important it was to keep all our buildings on a circuit; the property was too far away to constantly keep up with control. It was an outlier that required thought and planning to visit, oversee, and properly maintain. You really don't want that; you want something where all the routine stuff can be done on autopilot. You want to use your extra energy, efforts, and creativity on the big stuff, not waste it on the mundane. The Whittier property is where I learned that lesson.

And then out of the clear blue sky, a real estate broker approached me with a great offer to provide us with a 50 percent return on the buyout. His offer was pure luck; a joint venture purchaser was attempting to buy several apartment houses on the block. We immediately took him up on it—and you can see how it met our needs and his, and in no way did I resent that he was going to make money on the property after the sale—and we now had $75,000 to invest.

Now here's where understanding tax implications plays such a big part: From the Whittier sale, we would have been required to pay income tax that not only included the tax on gains, but also the tax on recapture of depreciation. So what we did was immediately start looking around for a larger property to comply with IRS 1031 Section exchange to avoid any capital gains tax.

In the hunt for a larger property, our broker found a fifty-two-unit property for sale in Temple City, the

Longden property. There was a tremendous upside to the property, which had been neglected. I knew with our approach, we could unlock a lot of potential. Plus, we knew that the Los Angeles County rent control it had been operating under was to end. This would mean a sizeable rent increase to come from the new rent schedule. We could make significant money on this property.

But financially it was out of our league.

The property had four individual owners and they owed a large first trust to the original owner/builder. Making an offer with a relatively low down payment of 7 percent was ridiculous, right? But we put together what we call "Constructive Financing."

I want to take a moment here to underscore the fact that our financing plan did NOT involve the owners lowering the selling price. This is all about working together so that everyone is happy. We were going to be asking the sellers to put a lot of faith in us despite the relatively small amount we could put down. You can't ask for that kind of flexibility and also expect them to lower their price.

In addition, there would be other potential buyers for the property who *did* have the money for a sizable down payment, and they would almost certainly be asking the sellers to lower their sales price. Because we agreed to their asking price, we suddenly looked more attractive than these other guys who would be trying to talk them down. You have to have something to offer. What we offered was a willingness to give them full price on the deal.

What we didn't have was the money, at least not up front. Here's what our Constructive Financing offer looked like; note that each aspect of the financing was approached step by step to win all the stakeholders over on our crazy offer.

- First, the brokers and management group were approached. We asked them not to waive their commissions, but to let us pay their commissions in six months. They accepted. This had to be the first step, because if they refused, we wouldn't be able to move forward. But also because once they had accepted, it would put them on our side. We then could proceed with the next step.

- Second, the four investors were approached to let us pay off their equity in two years. They accepted based on our good credit and the brokers' recommendations.

- Third, we asked the first trust owner to keep their high-interest loan in place for us. They accepted.

All parties were satisfied! It was necessary to make sure everyone involved could understand how they would benefit from the transaction. Each party in the acquisition had something. It was important to give the broker and management company their commission because they depended on the money. I don't work for free, you shouldn't work for free, so why should they work for free? The fact that we were willing to pay the initial sales price also meant that their commission, when they did get it, would be higher than if they worked with someone who wanted to negotiate down. Having the four investors keep their equity for two years was actually a big plus for them. It gave them time to reposition their investments and be prepared to report the sale of the property. And again, they were getting their asking price, which was certainly more than they would have expected to get with anyone else. Meanwhile, the first trust deed holder remained the same. Remember that he had nothing to gain by the sale of the property; in fact, if he was cashed out, it would upset his previous installment sale, creating a capital gains tax.

We bought the property and we kept our word on all fronts. We paid the brokers' commissions and all junior loans were paid off as agreed within two years. It is crucial to keep all agreements and make sure your creditworthiness stays intact. The cash flow to pay back everything was subsidized by the rent increases.

In the third year, market interest was lowered. We took the opportunity to negotiate with the first trust deed holder for a lower interest rate. In the fifth year, the market interest rate went even lower, so we negotiated again to lower the rate on the note.

Now to the fun stuff. Making any property more valuable is an exciting challenge, and I loved working on Longden. The process of making this particular property of greater value was to do major improvements.

The property was a two-story building with two flights of stairs, one on each end. This created considerable traffic between the staircases. To alleviate the traffic, a center staircase was installed. In addition, this provided more privacy because you didn't constantly have people walking past the center units. These are the kinds of things that aren't immediately obvious, but the beauty of it is you don't have to be a mind reader. Just go talk to the tenants. Find out what their pet peeves are. If you hear something at least three times, you know it's a thorn in everyone's side.

Back to improving the property.

In the back of the property there was open space. We developed a children's area there, plus we added a basketball court and a picnic area. There was also room to create garages that could accommodate motor homes, and there was even additional space to build storage rooms.

Once we tackled these major additions to the outside, the next area of major improvements was to renovate the interior of the apartments. As I mentioned earlier, putting in the newest, most water-saving fixtures doesn't just make the apartments more attractive; it saves on water and maintenance. You don't want to put in cheap stuff just because you yourself don't live there. For us, that wouldn't be living up to our motto, which is about our apartments being the best they can be, but it's also a very false economy. Cheap stuff breaks. The cost to you in maintenance and replacement parts—not to mention the hassle of it all—will vastly outstrip putting good quality stuff in there to begin with. Plus, that kind of thing spirals, and the next thing you know, no one wants to live in your buildings—and they certainly won't want to pay top dollar for them.

Here's what we improved upon: In the kitchens and bathrooms, we installed new cabinets and tile, while all fixtures were upgraded. In the entire apartment, we put in modern flooring. Wall-to-wall carpet with tile in the dining rooms so that our apartments visually popped. We stood out from the competition. New coats of paint, and everything looking top-notch.

Now, I am not suggesting you throw money at the place willy-nilly. The trick in all of these improvements was to do a cost-benefit analysis first. Could the improvements be justified with additional income, considering the cost? A ratio of return had to be justified within three years. But we also purchased a place where this kind of return could absolutely happen. The property was under-maintained. There was a lot of potential value there to be unlocked.

You also need to factor in how improvements can help your internal expense control. You want properly placed lighting with today's energy-efficient, long-lasting bulbs to provide safety and keep the cost of electricity at minimum. Shortage of water has become a premium consideration, especially here in Los Angeles. Changing from wasteful watering sprinklers to the most efficient, newer systems is a no-brainer. Keeping up with any leaks by immediately patching them is more economical than going for a new roof, but you can only do that by staying on top of things as they happen. Deferred maintenance does not mean ignoring the property—it means catching little things and fixing them early so that you can safely put off a major expense. We're retrofitting all of our buildings to the highest current standard of earthquake safety. It's expensive, but it will make the properties more valuable, and besides that, it's the right thing to do. Think long term.

Landscaping was another area in which to improve the property. Good landscaping provides street appeal for prospective tenants. When rents go up, you will always lose a few tenants for whom a low price is more important than an improved living space. That's okay.

You want tenants who want to live there and who want to take care of the property. But it means you will always be looking to attract new tenants. Even when you're full, you want to be seen as a place where people aspire to live.

I've talked about flowers and their importance to me, so you won't be surprised that we not only installed flowering bushes along the building, but also planted flowers in front of the bushes. We're lucky in Los Angeles that with the proper planning, something can be in bloom nearly every month of the year.

Out went the big trees. The root systems can cause significant damage, and besides, they were too big for the building's size. We replaced them with smaller trees that suited the property. We placed a fountain and ornaments around the property to give it a sophisticated look, and we added paths so that people could get where they needed to go without walking on the lawn.

Landscaping is always a work in progress. Even when you're providing the correct soil, ideal watering, the right combination of sun and shade, and the best plants for the area, you still need to give your landscaping regular attention. This is one of the reasons you want your properties on a circuit, because when you find the right landscaping company for your needs, you want to use them for everything. Training new people to do things your way should be avoided whenever possible.

But sometimes, it's not possible to go with what's at hand. I always hire a new manager when I take over a building because I'm very particular. I want things done a certain way. And while it's difficult to train a new manager, it's impossible to retrain an existing manager to do things differently. You also won't get the hire right every time. During the first several years at Longden, our on-site managers had to be changed more than once. Finding the right managers to suit the property is difficult. They are the eyes and ears of the rental properties and must pass on the problematic activities to the administrative staff. They have to be loyal to the owner while at the same time mindful of the needs of the tenants and the importance of keeping them satisfied. All-around goodwill is an important asset for the property manager.

Insurance policies for fire and liability were negotiated for best value of coverage. Just because you need these things doesn't mean you shouldn't shop around and use your best negotiating tactics. Everything matters. Finally, if you're able to do so, employing in-house painters, maintenance staff, and office staff will smooth out the entire running of the apartment houses. Once again, it's a question of training and making sure there are competent people whom you trust in every position.

Do you have to care this much to invest in real estate? No. Being a real estate investor can be done as a speculator. You can flip a building the same way you can flip a house by getting a good purchase price for the property, doing some cosmetics, and then selling it to someone else for a quick profit. But that's not our approach. It's a short-term view, whereas our approach in owning a residential income property is to see it as a long-term business. All improvements and maintenance are not quick fixes because that's not where the value lies. A greater success comes from visualizing the potential and then following through on that vision.

Just being productive is a great joy. The satisfaction of being a creative owner and putting your time and energy into making something wonderful—that is very rewarding, personally as well as financially. In time, a strong cash flow develops as you're getting top rents and paying off your most expensive debt. Then the funds to accelerate payments on the note for a full pay-off become available, making a huge difference to your cash flow.

With Longden, all of this was accomplished within ten years. Over that same period of time, there were ups and downs in the economy, of course, including times when people were unemployed and couldn't pay rent, and times when inflation meant we could raise the rent. Now we are seeing this building yielding 300 percent return year after year.

Being a landlord is a calling. We provide more than just a roof for our tenants; it is their home. And we make money doing it. People think that to thrive in business, you have to be heartless. Not at all! As a landlord, it is your responsibility to provide a decent living space. You have to stay educated on all the elements of financing, zoning laws, and regulations and codes from the city all the way up to the federal government. The potential of the property is not unlocked if you're providing subpar housing or skirting legal requirements. When you provide a wonderful experience to tenants, you are encouraging them to take care of the property. You're drawing to you the people who have the same values you do, and that ends up providing a win for everyone.

# Buyer's Remorse

When you've made the purchase, pop the champagne, celebrate with your loved ones, and get ready for the hard work. Don't second-guess yourself. You're never going to be totally happy; there's no such thing as the perfect deal, and in addition to that, you're human. You probably made some mistakes. Learn from them and let it go.

Fear is the great thing that will stop you in life. You can read this book, you can read a thousand books, you can learn at a mentor's feet, and you can still be too afraid to get started. But what are you afraid of? It's much smarter to address those fears, to look at the real worst-case scenario, and then to build in just enough of a safety net that the worst is still something you can live with.

You learn by doing. Stretch yourself. Push to make it happen. Don't make things harder by insisting that you must find the perfect property or that you must do everything flawlessly—or that you have to wait until the perfect time in the future. There is no perfect time. There are so many things you have to learn to do that aren't even on your radar (Maintenance! Taxes! Getting new tenants!) until you've gotten your feet wet. Your first property purchase is going to be difficult no matter when you do it. It's also not a lifetime commitment, it's not forever. Once you give it a try, you may decide you hate being a landlord. That's okay. You can always sell. But if you don't take the first step, you'll never know.

I took two years to find my first property. I drove around neighborhoods; I made sure there was sufficient traffic so enough people would see the "For Rent" signs; I checked for too much traffic or other noise pollution; I did a cost-benefit analysis on every potential property. I started out wanting a duplex, only to realize that a four-unit and then ultimately an eight-unit property actually made the most financial sense.

I'm not saying don't do your homework. I'm just saying don't take too long.

My daughter Ann has said that she'd title this book *No Fear*, because that's how I live my life. I like that. I think the real trick is not to add emotional baggage to your mistakes. I don't dwell on mine—I just handle them and move on. Make mistakes, fail small, get better. Don't let fear force you to live your life on the sidelines.

# RECAP: INVESTING IN REAL ESTATE

- **Have a plan.** Know what you want to buy and don't compromise.

- **Location is everything.** You never want to pay a premium for a location that can't get better, and you certainly don't want to be stuck in a location that will never improve.

- **Red flags are there to warn you.** Don't get so caught up in the idea of ownership that you fail to notice the two-hour commute, the lack of sunlight, or the significant structural problems.

- **Create value for your tenants.** Make your buildings stand out.

- **Negotiations are about being fair and setting your own limits.**

- **There is an art to putting the money together.** Be willing to be creative and to tap into every resource you have.

- **Unlocking potential is your greatest asset.** Look for places that have been underserved by their previous owner, and have a long-term view of the investments you make in the property.

- **Get your feet wet.** There will never be a perfect time.

# CHAPTER NINE

## DIVERSIFICATION

Diversifying your portfolio isn't just about making sure you're invested in more than tech stocks—although that's a good idea, too. Having too much of anything is asking for trouble. But real diversification is making sure that if one part of your wealth disappeared tomorrow, you wouldn't lose your house. Does this sound drastic? It happens. There are people who do, in fact, have nothing but tech stocks. When that bubble bursts, they are suddenly without savings and resources. Investments in other countries can vanish in the space of a regime change. More commonly, there are people—a lot of people—who have one job or sometimes a whole career with just one employer, and that employer suddenly goes bankrupt. Not only are they now without a paycheck, but they may also be without a pension they'd been counting on.

Don't put all your eggs in one basket. If wealth is independence, then dependence on any one source of wealth is the opposite of that. It yokes you to the vagaries of events you cannot always control. You need to think in broader terms and multiple pathways.

## Building on Your Strengths

I talked in Chapter Seven about leveraging your expertise by finding projects where you can trade sweat equity for partnership. I've done it many times, some fruitfully, some less so. But each time, I've learned something important. I highly recommend finding some way to get in on the ground floor of something by contributing your expertise rather than capital. If you can, it's a low-risk way to build out your relationships, your reputation, and your own abilities, and to become involved in something that could potentially have large financial rewards. In addition, your expertise can be the foundation of a side consulting business that can keep some money coming in if the day job abruptly ends.

But you have other strengths besides your expertise. Think about what else you do well. Maybe you're terrific at connecting other people; if so, that's a great skill. Be deliberate about it. Think of ways that you can get like-minded people together, be on the lookout for friends who need the skills of other friends. Becoming known as a connector makes you the first call when someone has a job opening—and maybe it'll be a job you yourself want to fill. Being the connector also means that you are helping your network in win-win situations, matching people who need a service with people who can provide that service. This builds a lot of goodwill and ensures that when you need help, you'll have a list of people happy to return the favor and connect you to their own resources.

A strength like this doesn't translate directly into income, but it can be parlayed into a new job or partnership opportunity. Other strengths, such as the ability to judge character, can help you hire the right people and save you both money and headaches in the long run. Or maybe you write great press releases even though you have no desire to go into public relations. Never dismiss something that you do well just because it doesn't immediately fill the coffers. Look for ways to use it and get even better at it. Put it in service of others. The contacts you can make by volunteering on a board, for instance, and being smart, sane, and useful there can lead to interesting and lucrative projects down the line.

## Avoiding the Hamster Wheel

Sure, diversifying your work is important because you want to have multiple income streams and a wide number of connections across industries. Both of those are key components to recession-proofing your career and your bank account. But you also want a diverse field of interest, because without it, you can get stuck in the hamster wheel, spinning forever and going nowhere.

I get bored easily. If there are no more challenges to a job, I move on. To some people, this makes no sense. If you have mastered a job, why not stay at it—now that it's easy, now that you can coast? For some people, that's the dream. But to me, that's exactly what makes it immoral for me to stay. I can't invest in something if I'm coasting. I can't do a "masterful" job when I'm bored. Being stuck on a hamster wheel does no favors to either you or your employer: You stop growing (bad for you) and you stop caring (bad for them). The only thing to do is leave and try something new.

Having diverse interests or adding new responsibilities to your current job can help you continue to grow, improve, and learn new skills, all of which keep the hamster wheel at bay. Or, if you do need to leave, it provides opportunities for new challenges to walk into. As I'm wrapping up this book, I just started a travel agency for package trips to Italy. I can hear you gasp from here: "A travel agency! Those things have gone the way of the dodo!" And while that is true in the larger sense, I believe there's opportunity for a niche company. I'm passionate about Italy, I have a lot of contacts there, and I want to share it with others. The fun I'm having doing something new is well worth the small financial risk I'm taking.

What does this have to do with being wealthy? First of all, I define true wealth as independence, and nothing could be less independent than being stuck in a hamster wheel where you stagnate. But also, our ability to create wealth comes from our engagement with the world. Making ourselves more valuable by taking on new challenges has a direct impact on our ability to make more money down the line. Investing in yourself doesn't just mean getting a college degree or putting your savings into your own business. It means investing in new skills, your marketability, and relationships. The hamster wheel may be comfortable, but it will sap all of these assets and leave you unprepared when something unexpected happens, or even when a new and better opportunity arises.

# The Vertical Path

There are two different paths you can take to enhance your wealth. Happily, this is not an either-or situation; in fact, you could and should take both. The real question is timing.

Early in your career, you will largely find yourself on the vertical path. This is where you are an apprentice, learning the craft, taking courses, working with mentors. Your goal at this stage is to grow your expertise in one area and move up the corporate ladder. This approach serves several worthy goals: You will gain experience in the field; you will find your strengths and build on your niche in this particular company; you will earn more money; you will develop higher-level contacts; and you will increasingly see more complex problems arising and being solved as you move up the ranks. All of these will serve you well as you build both your savings and your store of knowledge before you take the leap and run your own business.

In addition, when you do start out on your own, focus is critical. The vertical path there is in building a solid core business and not being distracted by every new opportunity that pops into view. There will be so much to do, so many details to take care of, so much to learn in those early years that a relentless focus on building up rather than out is essential. Our core business is real estate investment, and even now, when that part of the company is mature, it still demands a lot of time and care. Never allow your core business to suffer from neglect.

# The Horizontal Path

There is another path you should consider. When opportunity presents itself, consider transferring your skills into a different business. This is one of the ways in which having a large and diverse roster of contacts can make a real contribution to your life. You want to be able to reach out to people in different arenas to find out how what you're good at dovetails with what they need in industries outside your own. You may not use this information today or tomorrow, but at some point, you may want to make a move. Having those contacts and that know-how in your pocket makes everything much easier.

Just a reminder: When developing contacts, you want to share information both within your industry and across horizontal paths. It's a give-and-take; helping someone else learn the basics of your work world opens up channels into theirs. Beyond using the information to job-hunt in times of change, understanding how other businesses work gives you depth and a broad vision that can lead to making better decisions in your own business.

But later in your career, there will be another way to think of the horizontal path, and that is when you are building on your own success. This is the second path that you should take as you succeed and your core business solidifies. Where can you spin out from that core business into supporting industries?

The Barbera Conglomerate started with the apartment buildings. We owned them, we managed them, and once we had enough of them, it made sense to start building out. Not with physical buildings this time, but with the companies to service them.

Our service companies now include:

- Painting
- Maintenance
- Property management
- Marketing
- Restoration

You can see how these horizontal additions made perfect sense coming from our core business of owning apartment complexes. There are still things we outsource, of course. But everything we do is deliberate. We look at each situation and determine which is best: outsourcing or creating our own operation. I really consider the Barbera Conglomerate to be an investment company and a management group. Everything we do falls under that umbrella.

But we didn't stop with service companies. Our investments also orbit around our core business. Of course there's the investment in real estate with the buildings themselves, but we also got into the mortgage and insurance businesses. We started an investment company that purchases stocks, bonds, and other financial instruments. We follow our interests as well as our core expertise. Those interests include philanthropy. I started our foundation that supports primarily educational charities, but from that I spun off a publishing concern—which is how you're reading this book.

You can see how one interest naturally leads to another business opportunity. Because we have educated ourselves along the way in the things we needed to understand to run our core business, we were positioned to use that knowledge to help others. The horizontal path is taking the expertise you developed working on the vertical path and then spinning it out to invest in other businesses providing stability and multiple sources of income to your own portfolio.

This is a winning combination.

Here's how the horizontal path worked for me: When I bought my first property, I learned a lot about financing real estate. Of course, all of the other financial work I had been doing helped; I had a deep background in financing, so I was always able to see a way to raise the necessary money. I built equity with a passion and continued to parlay it into other properties.

Yet there was a limit to the amount of time I could devote to taking care of business. I had a demanding day job and I was doing most of the maintenance of the apartments, the painting, the landscaping, with my family on the weekends. I didn't even have time to check out new properties as they came on the market. It was Bernice who set me straight: If I wanted to reach the next level, I was going to have to commit fully to building our own businesses.

I stopped consulting for other people and put my entire focus on developing a management company. I also stopped painting walls and hired a professional painter. I stopped landscaping and hired professional gardeners. I spent my time on the analysis of potential properties and how to acquire them. But more important even than the focusing of my talents on something I loved and did well was the decision to start our family business. It was time to become an executive.

This was a crucial decision for me. I wanted to develop an ideal structure for a management company to take care of the different properties. I sized up how many units we'd need, and how many people, given a certain number of units, to manage everything—maintenance people, account staff, managers, landscapers, everyone. The number I hit on was 500 units. Now, understand that at the time, I had barely 100 units. But I realized that to maximize everyone's time and potential, 500 units would be an ideal number for our management company. Once I had that laid out, I put a plan in place and I was able to ideally move forward. I started to look at everything, every loan, every deal, from an executive point of view.

It was important for me to create a management company that could run even if I were no longer around. What incorporating did for me almost immediately was that it gave me a bigger picture, a larger vision that I was working for. When I found myself negotiating with anyone, from sellers to maintenance people to tenants, I was no longer just Robert Barbera wanting this concession or that job redone, I was in service of the management company. It was all business, not personal, and it wasn't about me, it was about building a company that would be an asset for my family for generations to come. And in fact, that's what has happened: The management company has been turned over to my children, and someday it will be my grandchildren's. A bigger vision can change your life.

Another critical component of our success was organization. It's incredible how much paperwork there is to do. Having a crackerjack staff is great, but having a solid plan to organize around is crucial to allow them to excel at their jobs. The skills you use when you're operating a management company are very different from the skills of owning and operating a single apartment building or even a handful of properties. It's about putting processes in place that other people can use to work at the highest possible level and keep everything running smoothly. This ladder concept could not have been achieved without the efficient organizing skills of my daughter Patty.

Look to see where you can grow not just by going up the ladder in your current work or bringing in more with your core business, but by diversifying within your area of expertise. Don't just climb up—spin out.

---

# CASE STUDY

## Captive Insurance

Captive insurance policies were developed to fill a need that general insurance companies were not offering. There are areas of coverage that are of unusual risk or out of mainstream coverage.

The Internal Revenue Service allows these types of insurance companies to be acknowledged as regulated insurance companies. It amounts to undertaking your special risk. We set up our own captive insurance company to underwrite our special requirements and grow financially as an insurance company.

---

## What Do You Still Need to Prove?

There comes a time in your life when you look pretty darn good on paper. The money is there, the family is doing well, and you have a nice car and a darn good title next to your name.

But if in your heart you wish for something more, or something completely different, then none of what you do have is real wealth.

Only you can know what that is. It can be a still-unrealized childhood dream, a creative passion, a particular accolade. I'm passing no judgments here, because what I think doesn't matter. The only thing that matters is that this thing, this missing piece, is keeping you from enjoying your wealth.

So do it.

Early on, I talked about how important it is to view yourself clearly, your strengths and weaknesses. It's also important to know your desires, what makes you happy. If you don't recognize the thing you need, you'll keep circling it. You'll waste time and energy flailing around, maybe even going after the wrong thing. If you still have something left to prove, think through what it is and then do it. Don't let an unfulfilled dream prevent you from enjoying the wealth you have earned.

If it's an action you can take—say, painting a beautiful seascape—then sign up for an art class, for crying out loud. Don't let anyone talk you out of it. There's nothing shameful about deciding to learn something new; on the contrary, that's how you stay on top of your game, by being willing to begin again somewhere. In business, I never resented taking a lower position in a new industry with high potential; this is exactly the same. Whether it's professional or personal, why should you ever feel bad about starting at the bottom if you're passionate about the possibilities? Don't let your ego or need to be top dog hold you back from living a full life.

Sometimes, it's a long-standing dream that you haven't made time for yet. For years, I had wanted to reconnect to my family's heritage. Going to Italy was a life-changing experience for me. Over the years, I've devoted some of my time and much of my creative energies into combating stereotypes of Italians and Italian Americans and spreading the word of their achievements. I have gotten tremendous personal satisfaction from these things; they have without question enriched my life. And now there's that new business venture on the horizon, giving me an opportunity to create wonderful travel experiences for others with a similar passion for Italy. I'm having the best time!

Or maybe there's something that signals success to you, and you haven't let yourself get it yet. There's nothing wrong with spending money on a symbol that allows you to fully feel successful. I'm not a materialistic fellow—Bernice and I spent years amusing ourselves by walking in the park, going to free concerts, and eating in. But when I made my first million, I splurged on a Jaguar. To me, that symbolized that I'd really made it. I still live below my means, but I also have that one thing that makes me feel like a million bucks.

There could also be a milestone that you still need to hit to feel like a winner. Early on, I determined that 500 units would be the ideal number for running an efficient, successful apartment rental operation. I hit it in the early 2000s. This wasn't directly related to any monetary goal; I just always felt this number would allow me to optimize all of our efforts and provide the greatest return on investment. Besides, it was a nice round number. For many reasons, it mattered when I hit it. If there's still something like that out there for you, what's stopping you? Don't let anyone tell you that it's a silly goal or that some arbitrary number doesn't matter. It does matter. It's your goal and your life. Why not go for it?

Finally—and this is the hardest one—maybe there's a regret. Maybe there's something you never tried for, a path you didn't take. And the problem with things like that is those opportunities are often gone for good. When I served in the National Guard, I started taking tests to become a second lieutenant. I quit halfway through. I was only eighteen at the time and I looked even younger; I was afraid the older soldiers would resent taking orders from me. And so I reined in what I knew I was capable of accomplishing so that I wouldn't have to deal with other people's hard feelings.

Boy, do I regret that.

The thing is—that ship has sailed. There is no way at this point in my life for me to become a second lieutenant. It also isn't something I want to do *now*—which doesn't mean I still don't wish I'd done it then.

There are two things you can do. First, you look at your life and see where you did the equivalent. I run my own business, I call my own shots. I've earned the respect of people older than me, even of mentors, many times in my life. The position of authority that I could have had, I have had in many other ways.

The other thing you can do is let it go. You made the best decision you could at the time. Don't let a past mistake rob you of the life you have now.

Let me end this with something my daughter Patty once said. She said that looking at my life, at how I've done so many different things, and different types of things—that, to her, is really exciting. She loves the idea that you don't have to be just one thing in your life. You can keep reinventing yourself.

I did, and you can, too.

# RECAP: DIVERSIFICATION

- **Don't put all your eggs in one basket.** If one stream of income vanished tomorrow, would the others remain intact? Having everything tied up in one arena invites disaster.

- **Build on your strengths.** You have expertise, but you also have other strengths. How can you use them to help others, build goodwill, and create new opportunities for yourself?

- **Challenge yourself.**

- **Tend the vertical path.** Do not neglect your core business.

- **Spin out onto the horizontal path.** Where does it make sense for you to launch a secondary company in support of your core business?

- **What's missing?** What do you still need to prove to yourself? Go ahead and prove it. It's your life.

# CHAPTER TEN

## REMAIN POISED FOR THE UNEXPECTED

I don't mean to scare you, but here's the truth: You can be a world expert, you can have a diversified portfolio and multiple streams of income, you can have a safety net, and things can still go terribly wrong. Here's another truth: You can rebuild. My parents went bankrupt twice and came back stronger both times. I've been fired, I've quit, I've been faced with challenges I didn't know how to overcome. Each time, I've gone to Plan B or Plan C, I've started over, I've even started at the bottom once again. It has never bothered me because I understand that it's all part of the process.

But being ready for the unexpected isn't about anticipating the worst—or at least not only about that. It's also about having a plan in place to take advantage of the new and exciting opportunities that will inevitably appear. You can't do that if you're wedded to only one way of doing things, or if you let your ego get in the way. If a new opportunity requires the loss of prestige or title, or necessitates going back to school or being terrible at a new skill for a while, why would you let an outer trapping like that get in the way of something that could propel you to new heights?

There are people who won't try something new because they tell themselves that at this stage of their career, it should be easy. The fact that something is challenging turns them off. I'm here to tell you that no matter where you are in your career, it's the challenges that you should be seeking out. People talk about retiring so they can do what they want. I am doing what I want. I am running businesses I enjoy with people I genuinely like and respect. I say, build your life so that you're doing what you want every day, and keep building it for as long as you're here on earth. Be ready for the next thing, and when it shows up, be willing to rise to the challenge.

---

# CASE STUDY

## Mortgages and Stocks

When the loan market and stock market bottomed out, the economy fell in a freefall. The "bubbles burst." It is lows like these that present opportunities to shift into a new business strategy.

We set up an administrative mortgage company to process real estate loans. The money to provide for loans came from our saved-up funds. My daughter Patty arranged various funds from our accounts. My son, John, and daughter Ann, along with my granddaughter Natalie, worked with brokers. We reached out to loan brokers to find a market, and we outsourced appraisers, a retired bank examiner, and escrow/title companies to do the remaining work. At the same time, we reorganized our cash flow to invest in the stock market low. We carefully reached out for a competent stock broker who fulfilled our expectation.

As we watched the pace of the two fields of investment, we slowed down on the mortgage market and moved on the stock market, which succeeded with less trouble and bigger returns.

There will always be new businesses popping up

and old industries dying off. If you started out life as a horse-and-cart maker, you'd better be able to learn how to fix bicycles, and then motor cars. When gold shot up in price, artisans who could only work in that medium found themselves closing up shop, regardless of their talent. It takes being flexible, not just talented.

It also takes recognizing that part of your job is always to be on the lookout for your next opportunity.

That opportunity may be a chance for a leadership role on a new project or a good place to reinvest some of your savings, or it might be learning a new skill or providing a service people don't even realize they need yet. You have to be on the lookout.

Read the financial news. Talk to a variety of people about their challenges and their needs. Keep an eye on the local real estate market. Be constantly learning, not just within your own field, but in related fields that are developing around your industry. Moving laterally can bring your skills into a new and exciting arena. Always be on the lookout for projects and people you can contribute to with little risk and a potentially strong back end.

Does this sound like a lot of work? When did I ever say growing wealth would be easy? The truth is that these things—being on top of business trends, honing your skills and seeing how they can be of value across industries, paying attention to investment opportunities, looking for ways to consult and trade your expertise for equity—these strategies are the bare minimum for acquiring wealth. You don't just show up at your day job and they flood you with money. You need to be better educated about your own field than anyone else in the room. You need to be able to connect the dots and see where trends are leading us. And you have to be willing to act.

Having said that, you also have to be willing to hit the pause button every now and again. I've leveled off in my own career from time to time. There are times when you're immersed in learning the ropes, and those times are not about stretching but about building a foundation. And there are just times when you need a break. I don't mean take a vacation—although my time in Italy was transformative—but I do mean that you don't have to push yourself every second. You can't keep up that pace and maintain your own physical and mental health. Beware addiction, and that includes the addiction to overwork. It's not wealth if it's driving you to an early grave.

## The Burden of Debt

At this stage of your life, I really want to encourage you to get rid of all debt. Living beneath our means was always our smartest move. There's a lot of stress in building wealth. When you are leveraging your investments and savings, you don't have a lot of room for error. There will always be some problem that costs a little more, or some opportunity if only you could stretch a little thinner, either with your money or with your energy and time. Being in debt makes it less likely that you'll be able to weather the sudden hiccup or take advantage of that great opportunity. Debt adds a burden of stress that keeps us from sleeping well, saps our energy and focus, and raises the stakes of every deal.

Why make it that much harder on yourself?

At every stage of your life, staying out of debt on a personal level is key. Once you've started to succeed, paying down debt, especially any high-interest loans, is critical. You need a certain amount of equity you are willing to leverage, but you also need a critical minimum in terms of peace of mind. Let me tell you, one of the happiest days of my life was only a decade or so ago, when I had finally paid off all that debt I'd been carrying for years. Patty was instrumental and facilitated the cash flow so we could reduce debt on the buildings. Now, when I have a vacancy, it's not a big deal. I'm not worried about filling it immediately. I mean, terror is a strong word, but there were times when a vacancy would skyrocket my stress levels. Now, I can feel peaceful. What a feeling! It takes discipline and sacrifice to cut back on your standard of living while you focus on becoming debt-free, but the real freedom—the real wealth—that becomes available once you are unburdened is tremendous.

Don't let debt strip you of flexibility and the energy you need to succeed. And don't pass that burden of debt along to your family should something happen to you.

## Real Freedom

What do I consider to be real freedom? It's independence, the ability to call your own shots, run your business the way you want to, and live your life to the fullest. You might notice that even when I worked for others, I always did things my own way. I lived up to my own values and my integrity, and I was constantly improving workflow and outcomes, whether I was running a restaurant, a credit union, or my own apartment complex.

There is another aspect to freedom, however, that you must take into account, and that is your health. Overwork and stress are common problems for entrepreneurs, including me. You are no good to anyone if you're in the ICU with a heart attack. That is not living your best life. So moderate. I know, it's easier said than done, but this is where building in a safety net really makes a difference. Train people to do things the way you want them done and outsource wherever possible. Hiring great help is a critical component of running a business. Hoarding your money by trying to do everything yourself does not make you rich, it gives you ulcers. Early on, yes, you'll need to do a lot yourself—for one thing, because you want to make sure you understand how everything should be done. You can't hire a great landscaper if you don't understand the work involved. But even then, get support. Involve your family, learn from experts, don't spread yourself too thin.

Speaking of family, real wealth is time, time to spend with those you love. I'm not much of a guy for hobbies—whatever my new venture is, that's my hobby—but it's always been important to me to spend time with my family.

## Continue to Have a Long Investment Horizon

I mentioned this when I talked about the stock market, the importance of thinking long term, but in fact, I have a long investment horizon in everything I do. The reason for it isn't just good business sense and a distrust of get-rich-quick schemes. When you build for the future, when you look to the long term, you take possession of and responsibility for your investment. You will do a better job, you will make better decisions, and you will have a better outcome because this is not some fly-by-night scheme you're trying, but something you care about. Building for the future makes you a better investor, no matter what stage of your life or career you happen to find yourself in.

## Invest Emotionally

Investing isn't just about money. I coached my kid's baseball team. I went door to door raising money for the YMCA. I used my expertise in stocks to help develop existing funds at two different colleges as a way to give back for the scholarship money I myself had received. Over the years, there have been a number of charities that I have worked with, including a pro-life organization that I helped found after the loss of our second child. These were not activities that required me to donate money, but they did require time. They required caring.

What do you care about? How can you invest emotionally in your community? I use the term "community" in the broadest possible sense. For whatever cause is dear to your heart, there is probably an organization out there to support it. And if there isn't, you could start one. You've benefited from mentors; whom can you help mentor now? How can you share your success? In your family, in your neighborhood, in your world, what can you do to make a difference? Investing emotionally has a different kind of return on investment than investing financially, but it's one that's no less important.

# Estate Planning

Here is another aspect of life where people fail to plan. But with this one, you won't get a do-over.

I can't tell you how important it is to plan your legacy while you're still alive. This shouldn't be depressing, but uplifting. Look at what you've accomplished! You have been fearless in building your business, so why should you be afraid to sit down and plan out what happens to it once you're gone? Estate planning is the greatest gift you can give your family. Don't let baseless fears keep you from the joy and peace that comes with knowing you have taken care of them.

This is an area where you need an expert. Financially, there are so many things to consider. You want to minimize estate taxes, you want to make sure any trusts have reliable trustees, and you want to make sure your documents cover every contingency. A trusted adviser with expertise in this field is priceless. Do not try to do it yourself.

There is, however, something you should do yourself, and that is talk to your heirs. Some people, sadly, see money as a substitute for love; leaving more to one person than another can be seen as playing favorites from beyond the grave. But the fact is that your estate may not neatly divide. Someone may get the family business while another gets the house, and if you don't address concerns and issues before the will is read, you sure won't get the chance to do it after. Talk to your family and business partners, make sure your wishes are known, but take their wishes and preferences into account as well.

You also want to take this time to give your heirs a sense of ownership and commitment to your family business. You want as seamless a transition as possible for everyone's benefit, and that can be greatly helped by bringing them into leadership positions while you're still around to guide them.

Finally, take the time to write a goodbye letter. Only you know who needs to receive it. There are things unsaid that need to be said. Now is the time to release and forgive, to close the book on the lingering resentments and troubles. Leaving peace for others may be your greatest gift.

# Beyond the Finances

When you think of your legacy, you should also think about the good you want to do in the world while you're still here. Think of philanthropy and community leadership as your living legacy. This is where that emotional investing hits home, but in addition to searching for where you can give of yourself and of your resources to do good in the world, look to see where you can pass on what you've learned and help others reach success. Think about how you want to be remembered. I'm going to guess it's not just for your money. We all have a need to belong and to matter. Honor this need in yourself by looking for ways to be active and helpful in the world.

For me, creating The Mentoris Project has been an important part of my legacy. Its mission is to advance the tradition of mentoring. We create books, both print and digital, recounting the achievements of Italians and Italian Americans. They aren't textbooks; they are inspirational books, primarily biographies and novels based on the lives of remarkable people. This dovetails with my interest in the culture of Italy and in making sure Italian Americans learn about our rich history. To date, Mentoris has commissioned more than thirty writers to write over fifty books, ranging from architecture to sports, exploration, music, and religion. To me, the power of storytelling offers a chance for people to put down one of our books after reading of someone's amazing achievements and say, "I could do something amazing, too." That's the power of a mentor, and I am honored to be able to bring inspiration to so many people through The Mentoris Project. It allows me to share my passion and is an important piece of my legacy. Now is the time in your life when you can dive into what really matters to you and offer it up to the world.

Having given something to the wider world, you should also look closer to home. How will your family have benefited from your life's work, beyond any financial legacy? Your children, your grandchildren? I can tell you, my grandchildren learn our business from the ground up. I make them paint an apartment so that they know how to manage painters. I have them fix things so that they know how to manage the maintenance workers. Every Barbera family member at some point has to manage an apartment building; it's not just a rite of passage, it is a training ground in handling the unexpected. I explain this to my kids and grandkids so that they understand the trust I'm putting in them. Just like with the stock market, it's all about educating yourself before the stakes get high. Someday this business will be theirs; I don't want them—and they don't want themselves—to suddenly find they're running a business they don't understand.

# CASE STUDY

## Publishing

The power of printing is enormous. It can be negative or positive. My fond hope was to recognize my heritage and pass it on. It started with becoming the publisher of an Italian American newspaper. From this success we developed The Mentoris Project. Fifty significant Italian and Italian American fictional biographies are now in production. The key to our venture was outsourcing: manuscript writers, editors, graphic artists, and a competent manager in charge.

This endeavor brought on huge excitement and challenges. Each day we are alive to accomplish a service to our community.

Think about this in terms of your own legacy. How can you provide a training ground to your heirs so that they can learn the basics of the business that you so painstakingly built? How can you transfer institutional knowledge and give them the hands-on experience needed to flourish? Don't do your loved ones the disservice of giving them an inheritance they are unprepared to handle.

# Retirement

Finally, there is something that's not unexpected, but you still have to be ready for it. That's retirement. I'm not a fan. In fact, I would never suggest that you retire. I remember how people used to announce their retirement and then be dead in a year or two. Retiring didn't bring them joy; it sapped their sense of purpose. Without the challenges of work, there was nothing left to live for. The unexpected here is not retirement itself, but the detriment it can cause.

I love working. I love every day and every new challenge. If you are ready to move on to a new challenge that doesn't involve the work you're doing now, then certainly retire from it, but have a plan in place before you do. If your heart's desire is to be the oldest person to climb Mt. Everest, I wish you well—and certainly I think you'll live longer doing that than you would spending time puttering around the house. Having too much time and too few goals, that's the real killer.

# RECAP: REMAIN POISED FOR THE UNEXPECTED

- **Changing landscapes are opportunities, but only if you clearly see them coming.** Stay on top of your industry and your investments.

- **Get out of debt to give yourself the flexibility to pivot.**

- **Family is the most valuable part of your life.** Involve them in your work and pave the way for them to successfully take over your business.

- **Have a long investment horizon in everything.**

- **Invest emotionally in your community and the issues you care about.**

- **Plan for when you are no longer here.** Take the time to heal what needs to be healed between you and the ones you love.

- **Continue to challenge yourself at every stage of your life.**

# CONCLUSION

## TRUE WEALTH

This book contains everything I can tell you about how to create wealth. Live beneath your means, sacrifice to save the funds for your first investment, leverage your skills and your successes, purchase potential not bragging rights, be honest and fair to everyone you meet and in every negotiation, bring your family into your business early, appreciate your loved ones, and contribute what you can to the world. These are the things that create a wealthy life.

But I don't want you to read this book and think that I never failed at anything. That's an impossible bar to aspire to, and it's simply not true. I've lost money in the stock market, I've purchased apartment complexes that I wasn't able to turn around, and I spent two whole years running a restaurant, which left me no time to spend with my family—one of the few mistakes I truly regret. Of course I make a wrong choice or have a bad day, but I don't dwell on it. I don't belabor it or beat myself up about it. Bad decisions are part of the cost of doing business. You need a cushion; you need to factor goofs into your financial planning and also into your conception of who you are and what life is. I make a point of learning from my mistakes and I hope you will, too, but don't let them keep you from moving forward.

I also celebrate success. It is very important to acknowledge milestones, whether it's your first client or your first million. Bernice and I always had fun, and we certainly celebrated when things went well. We just never spent a lot of money doing it. Have rituals that you and your loved ones do together to celebrate every win; just don't make them dinners out at the fanciest restaurant in town. Picnics were a favorite pastime with the Barbera family. I'm sure you can think of something relaxing and fun that works for you.

You should also have something that symbolizes success to you. Symbols mean a lot to us as human beings—in fact, I believe my wife, Josephine, and I can live as simply as we do, and as happily, because we have just a few symbols that resonate with us. We don't need everything drenched in diamonds; we don't have a butler, Josephine still cooks dinner, I still wash the dishes every night. For me, my car is my big splurge; driving a great car has always been the one thing that, to me, symbolized my success. But I still drive it while wearing good-quality, long-lasting clothes that never have—and never will—reflect the latest trends. I don't need to wear Gucci to feel like a million bucks.

Maybe cars do nothing for you; maybe your symbol is the view from your office or a beautiful painting or a letter acknowledging a major donation that you were able to make to something you care deeply about. Keep that symbol front and center and you won't need to waste your money on constant little reminders.

Speaking of reminders, this is a good time to remind you that you have something of value to give to others. Think of your living legacy, the good you still want to do. Nothing makes you feel wealthier than helping others or making a positive difference in the world. Look around for those you can help one-on-one, or see where you can shift the needle for good.

Finally, the one thing that true wealth really offers is time with the people you love. You have sacrificed together, built something worthwhile together, and celebrated together. That's the greatest wealth there is.

I hope this book has helped you to see the different pieces of the puzzle that must come together to build wealth and that you will have tremendous success on your own journey. I was casting about for some final words to give you, something that would tie it all together. In my own life, I have always been compelled to reach for that next accomplishment, but at the same time, I have always enjoyed every step along the way. Perhaps that's the real secret to wealth: Stretch yourself, go for the gold, but enjoy every bit of what you have right now.

I wish you wealth.

# About the Author

Robert Barbera is a proud Italian-American. His immigrant parents taught him the value of hard work and the importance of family. He made his first stock investment in 1954, only four years out of high school, and bought his first building in 1961. Through hard work, dedication, focus, and the support of his family, he now has 500 units and multiple subsidiary companies, making real estate the cornerstone of his success.

Throughout his life, Robert has built wealth not just for himself and his family, but for many other people in fields as diverse as restaurants, car dealerships, and the financial industry. He launched The Barbera Foundation in 1994 and has donated his time, expertise, and financial resources to many worthy organizations, including Pepperdine University, Thomas Aquinas College, and the California State University system.

Robert was lucky in love, having had a happy, forty-five-year marriage to his late wife, Bernice, and finding love a second time around with Josephine, whom he married in 2003. He is the father of three wonderful children, Ann, John, and Patricia, and the grandfather of seven.

The Mentoris Project represents a piece of Robert's legacy. It connects his past, his parents, his children, and the future by honoring the achievements of Italians and Italian-Americans and publishing inspirational books. Learn more at https://www.mentorisproject.org

# ACKNOWLEDGMENTS

Thank you to my Mother for teaching me to appreciate life and that "life is a bowl of cherries."

To my older brother Henry, who motivated me to expand my horizons by pushing me to go to college and then recognizing me as a real estate investor.

I am very blessed for having two wives in my lifetime.

I'm grateful for my beautiful marriage with Bernice, her love for our children, and our life-long partnership.

Thank you, Josephine, for loving me unconditionally.

Thank you to my children and grandchildren for being the motivation and drive for everything I do.

Thank you to Edward DeLoreto for encouraging me to become a philanthropist.

To my business associates, particularly Norman Sarafian and John Sinner.

To my dear friend Jim Gallo for reminding me of my heritage.

A special thanks to Michael Gourdikian for assisting me in most of my real estate purchases and negotiating the best terms.

My staff at Barbera Management, who are particularly notable.

To Ken LaZebnik and Dominic Pulera for inspiring me to start the Mentoris Project.

Thank you to my managing editor Karen Richardson for all your hard work and dedication to the Mentoris Project.

Thank you to Laura Brennan for doing such a beautiful job in bringing my life into this book.

Finally, thank you to my granddaughter Natalie for picking up the many pieces of varied interests.

# NOW AVAILABLE FROM THE MENTORIS PROJECT

*America's Forgotten Founding Father*
*A Novel Based on the Life of Filippo Mazzei*
by Rosanne Welch, PhD

*A. P. Giannini—The People's Banker*
by Francesca Valente

*The Architect Who Changed Our World*
*A Novel Based on the Life of Andrea Palladio*
by Pamela Winfrey

*A Boxing Trainer's Journey*
*A Novel Based on the Life of Angelo Dundee*
by Jonathan Brown

*Breaking Barriers*
*A Novel Based on the Life of Laura Bassi*
by Jule Selbo

*Building Heaven's Ceiling*
*A Novel Based on the Life of Filippo Brunelleschi*
by Joe Cline

*Building Wealth 101*
*How to Make Your Money Work for You*
by Robert Barbera

*Christopher Columbus: His Life and Discoveries*
by Mario Di Giovanni

*Dark Labyrinth*
*A Novel Based on the Life of Galileo Galilei*
by Peter David Myers

*Defying Danger*
*A Novel Based on the Life of Father Matteo Ricci*
by Nicole Gregory

*The Divine Proportions of Luca Pacioli*
*A Novel Based on the Life of Luca Pacioli*
by W. A. W. Parker

*Dreams of Discovery*
*A Novel Based on the Life of the Explorer John Cabot*
by Jule Selbo

*The Faithful*
*A Novel Based on the Life of Giuseppe Verdi*
by Collin Mitchell

*Fermi's Gifts*
*A Novel Based on the Life of Enrico Fermi*
by Kate Fuglei

*First Among Equals*
*A Novel Based on the Life of Cosimo de' Medici*
by Francesco Massaccesi

*God's Messenger*
*A Novel Based on the Life of Mother Frances X. Cabrini*
by Nicole Gregory

*Grace Notes*
*A Novel Based on the Life of Henry Mancini*
by Stacia Raymond

*Harvesting the American Dream*
*A Novel Based on the Life of Ernest Gallo*
by Karen Richardson

*Humble Servant of Truth*
*A Novel Based on the Life of Thomas Aquinas*
by Margaret O'Reilly

*Leonardo's Secret*
*A Novel Based on the Life of Leonardo da Vinci*
by Peter David Myers

*Little by Little We Won*
*A Novel Based on the Life of Angela Bambace*
by Peg A. Lamphier, PhD

*The Making of a Prince*
*A Novel Based on the Life of Niccolò Machiavelli*
by Maurizio Marmorstein

*A Man of Action Saving Liberty*
*A Novel Based on the Life of Giuseppe Garibaldi*
by Rosanne Welch, PhD

*Marconi and His Muses*
*A Novel Based on the Life of Guglielmo Marconi*
by Pamela Winfrey

*No Person Above the Law*
*A Novel Based on the Life of Judge John J. Sirica*
by Cynthia Cooper

*Relentless Visionary: Alessandro Volta*
by Michael Berick

*Ride Into the Sun*
*A Novel Based on the Life of Scipio Africanus*
by Patric Verrone

*Saving the Republic*
*A Novel Based on the Life of Marcus Cicero*
by Eric D. Martin

*Soldier, Diplomat, Archaeologist*
*A Novel Based on the Bold Life of Louis Palma di Cesnola*
by Peg A. Lamphier, PhD

*The Soul of a Child*
*A Novel Based on the Life of Maria Montessori*
by Kate Fuglei

*What a Woman Can Do*
*A Novel Based on the Life of Artemisia Gentileschi*
by Peg A. Lamphier, PhD

# FUTURE TITLES FROM THE MENTORIS PROJECT

*A Biography about Rita Levi-Montalcini*
and
Novels Based on the Lives of:
*Amerigo Vespucci*
*Andrea Doria*
*Antonin Scalia*
*Antonio Meucci*
*Buzzie Bavasi*
*Cesare Beccaria*
*Father Eusebio Francisco Kino*
*Federico Fellini*
*Frank Capra*
*Guido d'Arezzo*
*Harry Warren*
*Leonardo Fibonacci*
*Maria Gaetana Agnesi*
*Mario Andretti*
*Peter Rodino*
*Pietro Belluschi*
*Saint Augustine of Hippo*
*Saint Francis of Assisi*
*Vince Lombardi*

For more information on these titles and the Mentoris Project, please visit
www.mentorisproject.org

Made in the USA
Columbia, SC
07 February 2025

53458796R00121